The Angels of the First Heaven

The Angels of the First Heaven

How to work with the Seven Archangels

Carolyn Gilbody Bowyer

illustrated by Nikki Julienne Isaac

BOOKS

Winchester, U.K.
New York, U.S.A.

First published by O Books, 2007
O Books is an imprint of John Hunt Publishing Ltd.,
The Bothy, Deershot Lodge, Park Lane, Ropley,
Hants, SO24 0BE, UK
office1@o-books.net
www.o-books.net

Distribution in:

UK and Europe
Orca Book Services
orders@orcabookservices.co.uk
Tel: 01202 665432
Fax: 01202 666219 Int. code (44)

USA and Canada
NBN
custserv@nbnbooks.com
Tel: 1 800 462 6420
Fax: 1 800 338 4550

Australia and New Zealand
Brumby Books
sales@brumbybooks.com.au
Tel: 61 3 9761 5535
Fax: 61 3 9761 7095

Far East (offices in Singapore, Thailand,
Hong Kong, Taiwan)
Pansing Distribution Pte Ltd
kemal@pansing.com
Tel: 65 6319 9939
Fax: 65 6462 5761

South Africa
Alternative Books
altbook@peterhyde.co.za
Tel: 021 447 5300
Fax: 021 447 1430

Text copyright Carolyn Bowyer 2007

Design: Jim Weaver

ISBN-13: 978 1 84694 015 6
ISBN-10: 1 84694 015 X

A CIP catalogue record for this book is available from the
British Library.

Printed in the US by Maple Vail

Acknowledgements

I would like to thank all the people who have helped me with this book. Particularly, my husband Bo and my daughter Nikki Julienne Isaac and Val Lavelle who painstakingly read through and corrected any grammar mistakes! To all my friends and all those who have attended my workshops.

May the angels bless you all.

Most of all I would like to give thanks to the angels, who have supported and pushed me gently along this path and have held me up whenever I felt like giving up!

Contents

Introduction

"What happens when you die, Daddy?" I asked my father when I was a young child. My father was rather taken aback by this question, but never a man to be hurried, he thought carefully before replying, "I don't really know. I guess you just fade into nothingness." I was appalled!

"No Daddy, that can't possibly be!" I waved my arms around my head and my heart, and pointing to both I said, "What I have here can't die!"

My father was so amazed by what I had said that he began to talk to his customers, friends, and people he met. Some of them must have confirmed my belief, for he began to bring home articles and books to read to me that confirmed it.

Amongst them was a story about a man named Edgar Cayce, it was called *There is a River* by Thomas Sugrue. The first part of the story told how Edgar had met up with an angel as a child. He had asked for help with his homework, and the angel had told him that he must put the book he wanted to remember under his pillow at night, and in the morning he would know all of it! I never tried doing this but I did wish that I could meet with an angel. When it did happen to me, I was so surprised and overwhelmed I found I couldn't tell anyone for a long time. Several years in fact.

Would you like to have an angelic experience? They are more commonplace than you would think. When I started teaching my workshops in 1997, I found people from all walks of life came to me with their stories, and they were all very different. What was the same about them all was that they had all had a profound effect on their lives. One woman told me, on seeing the painting of Uriel that she had seen him standing at the top of the stairs when she was a child and had always wondered who he was. It was not until she saw the painting that she knew and she was in her sixties when I met her.

Another woman told me how she had awoken one night to find an angel standing in her bedroom. "She was all gold and glittery," she said, "And I was so amazed that I could not speak to her or ask why she was there, but I know it was my guardian angel. I felt so wonderful for days!"

If you do meet up with your angel, it's wise to do your best to remember to ask who they are and what they want with you!

Angels are helping us to change our world for the better and to help us find ourselves, understand ourselves and totally become ourselves. The more I work with them the more I find myself capable of doing! I am also more content and at peace with myself than I have ever been.

Sometimes when I see the strife in some people's lives, and their unhappiness, it breaks my heart. For I know that if they asked the angels for help, the angels would give them the strength they need to overcome their problems.

One lady I know who asked the angels to help her find a new home, was amazed how quickly it all happened. She lived in the poorest housing and had tried to sell but no one had even come to look at the house. When she asked the angels for help, her house was sold in two days! She then had nowhere to go but the next day she received news of a house that looked as if it would suit her. When she went to see it, the house was just perfect for her and her family. A relative then came and offered the money she needed to make the house hers!

I often ask the angels how to help people become more aware of their existence and this book is one of the ways I was given. I have enjoyed writing it. I hope you enjoy reading it.

Carolyn Bowyer
September 2005

How to use this book

In each of the seven chapters on the archangels you will find instructions about working with that particular angel. You will find suggestions that you use a certain number of candles of a particular colour, oils to use on a burner, crystals to have present and water and essences to drink. If you need more information on where to obtain some of these, see the information on stockists at the end of this section.

Gather together all the things you need, such as the appropriate coloured crystals and candles. If you have a cloth the colour of the angel's ray use that to cover your table. If you do not have anything of that colour then use white or gold. You will need an oil burner in which to place the appropriate oils for the angel you wish to focus on. You do not need to use all the oils stated, you can use just one or two. If you like you can send to me for the appropriate angel oil (address at the end of this section) or make your own.

For the colour charged water, you need to find a glass or bottle of the appropriate colour and fill with water and then place it in the sun for at least 30 minutes. If it is not a sunny day you need to leave it for about an hour in the light or wait until it is sunny. Underneath the water put some paper with words such as, "This water is charged with energy of the Archangel ......" putting the name of the angel you wish to work with. Why do this? It has now been proved by the work of Japanese scientist Dr Masaru Emoto that water can and does take on the pattern given to it. Water also has a memory. So as you put your water in the sun, tell it that it is beautiful angelic water with the energy of the particular angel you wish to work with. If you have a torch with various colour discs, you can use this to charge the water, using the correct colour for the angel you have chosen to focus on. If you own an Isis pendulum you can use it to charge your water with the colour you need. The ruby gold is the hardest to deal with so you need to get creative; get some glass paint in the appropriate colours, find a clear bottle and paint away! I was lucky that I found one with real gold in it in Malta at Mdina glass, but it's a bit expensive to travel to Malta just to get a bottle! You will notice when you drink the different charged waters that they all have a different taste. You can also use these waters to help your health; blue charged water for instance is very good for soothing a sore throat. If you wish, you can purchase the appropriate angel essence and lace your water with it as well. (See at the end of this section for addresses.)

The number of candles you need varies with the different angels. If you do not have the number stated, don't worry, as long as you have at least one in that particular colour it will do. Just make sure you light it and that you use it safely.

If you have the crystals stated in the appropriate chapter then use them, if you do not, but have crystals of the appropriate colour, then use them. If you do not have any of the right colour then use quartz if you have it. Quartz always enhances everything you do.

You will also need to have to hand the picture of the angel you wish to focus on. When you actually do the focus, keep your eyes open and concentrate on the picture and ask the angel you are concentrating on to come through to you. Some of them will change dramatically. Gabriel becomes a baby then an old man, then changes again, it's fascinating to watch. Keep your eyes open as long as you can, until you feel you cannot keep them open any more, then close your eyes and go with the resonation. Remember to really feel the energy that's coming through to you, and concentrate on how it makes you feel.

You will also need appropriate music to play during the time you focus on the picture. I would strongly recommend you buy Neil H's *Resonation of Angels*, as this was specially recorded for this purpose. It is different to most angel music as it was channelled and recorded at a special workshop that Neil and I did together in 2002. Neil plays music that actually resonates the angel's name. Many people that attended the workshop had amazing angelic experiences that night and I myself saw the angel thrones for the first time.

With some of the focuses you will also need to write things down before you begin, namely Archangel Zadkiel and Archangel Michael. Destroy the pieces of paper safely afterwards.

If you can carry out Raphael's focus outside, do so. Raphael likes to be near trees and flowers and it's just so nice to be out in the fresh air.

Before you begin it also advisable to cleanse your aura. There are specific aura cleansers you can use. I make angel essence sprays for this purpose; you can make your own or use one of the oils suggested, but the angel essence sprays appear to be the most effective, and the feedback I am getting about them is truly amazing.

Cleanse your aura by putting some into your hands and rubbing them together. Then lift your hands up over your face and head, keeping them about 6 to 10 inches away from your skin. Bring your hands down around your body moving from front to back, so that your hands touch at the back. Go down as far as you can reach and then place both hands on the ground.

I always suggest chanting and singing to build up the energy before you begin. The angels' vibrations are higher than yours are, and you need to raise your vibration to enable the angels to come through more easily. I have given you ideas on the chants to use, and the music is available on CD which you can obtain from me if you wish. If you feel you cannot sing, I suggest you sing with your mind. I had a white rose bush in my garden which when it flowered only had a few blooms. I decided to sing to it, but as my garden is overlooked, I felt I could not sing out loud as the neighbours might think me nuttier than usual! So I sang to the rose with my mind. I sang an old Cornish song that goes something like, 'I love the white rose in her splendour, I love the white rose as fair as she grows.' I don't know any more of the words, but I sang this to the bush regularly, and that year it produced over 100 blooms. I also find that when you are singing in your mind you can sing a lot better and with more passion. Try it! You may use singing bowls if you wish. These are metal bowls, usually made in Tibet, that when you rub round the outside edge with a small wooden stick, produce a high note vibration.

Here is a summary of the things you need

- Cloth to cover table used.
- Candles of appropriate colour.
- Crystals of appropriate colour.
- Water to drink charged with correct colour and essence.
- Oil burner and correct oils.
- Songs to sing.
- *Resonation of Angels* CD and CD player.
- Paper to write on for Michael and Zadkiel.
- Possibly singing bowls.
- Angel picture.
- Aura Cleanser – Angel Essence spray.

Set everything up and then:
1. Light the candles.
2. Cleanse your aura.
3. Drink the water and essence.
4. Put the oils on the burner.
5. Sing your chants.
6. Play the resonation.
7. Focus on the picture.
8. Ask your particular angel to come through.

Afterwards allow yourself to settle and then write down your experience. If you felt nothing at all try again another day. Perhaps this all sounds like too much trouble, but the more effort you put in, the better your results are likely to be. The angels too, really appreciate us making an effort to please them.

One last thing, remember to thank the angels for their help.

Supplier's addresses

For Angel Oils, Angel Essences, Angel Essence Sprays, Angel Cards, Angel Chant CD called *Angels Present* etc. contact:

Carolyn Bowyer
The Angel Lady of Cornwall
65 Porth Bean Road
Newquay
Cornwall TR7 3JD
01637 873024
www.cornwallsangel.co.uk

For the *Resonation of Angels* CD and the *Resonation of the Angels of Second Heaven* (due to be released in Nov 06)
Neil H Music
33 Cramber Close, Belliver Estate
Plymouth
Devon PL6 7AZ
www.neilhmusic.co.uk

For beautiful crystals contact
Barrie and Nina Williamson
Cornerways
The Cross
Carlton in Lindrick
Notts S81 9EW
01909 733761

I

The Hierarchy of the Angels

When I first came across the hierarchy of angels, the number of different angels there were surprised me. At first I felt that I had only dealt with the guardian angels and the archangels, but as I looked into it further I realized that I had often been aided by many of the others.

I was to discover that there are many angels, called by many different names according to whichever religion you looked at. The Christians, the Jews and the Muslims all have their own ideas on angels, although many ideas are believed by all three, Gabriel for instance is accepted as an angel by all three. The Hindus have devas and the

Japanese have angel-like beings in their mythology. There are many references the whole world over to beings that could be thought of as angels.

Angel actually comes from a Greek word that means messenger, and this is what they mainly do for us. They do their best to bring messages that encourage us to take the right path and increase our self-respect. They support us through bad times and help us keep the light within us shining.

However the only order of angels that appealed to me personally was one put forward in the Celestial Hierarchy that was seemingly written by Dionysius the Areopagite. Although these writings bear his name, it is believed an unknown Alexandrian of the early 6th century BC probably wrote them.

Seeking more information and clarification on these matters, I decided to consult with the angels themselves. As Jophiel is the archangel of wisdom, I felt that he was the best one to ask. Jophiel is also a very joyful angel and so when I asked him about the hierarchy I was not surprised when he started to laugh.

He explained that there are no such things as hierarchies as such in their dimension, all are accepted as powerful in their rightful place.

"Hierarchies" he told me "are a thing from the human dimension." He went on to say that there are many different kinds of angels and that each is very important in their own way.

"Think!" he said "the food you eat is very important, you need different amounts of protein, fat and carbohydrate and you also need vitamins and minerals. You need only very small amounts of vitamins, but this does not make them any the less important than the other nutrients."

"When a spirit is ready to take on the role of 'angel' the spirit itself is aware of its own evolution and it knows which role it is ready to accept. It is much akin to when you choose a career on your plane, you then go about getting the right qualifications to do that particular job, in our plane it is when you know in yourself that you are ready to take on that role, that you actually become it. It is always your choice however, there is no pressure."

"So does this mean," I asked "that all of these angels in this hierarchy do not exist?"

"They exist! It is just that none are really recognized as being better than another, however as our spirits evolve then we become what you in your dimension regard as a higher being. Thus if I felt ready to become a Seraph, then I would become a Seraph, another would take my role as the Archangel Jophiel."

"Do you want to become a Seraph?"

"No! I am happy to be who I am! I only used that as an example. I am most suited to my role, I would not choose to be Michael, nor would he choose to be me. We are both perfect in our own roles. The Seraphim are truly amazing but where I am in my own evolution I am perfect. In fact we are all perfect! Yes even you! Where we are at this moment in time is the perfect place for us to receive the lessons we need to learn. So whilst you on the human plane call it a hierarchy, we on this plane do not see it that way. All of the angels in your hierarchy exist and many more besides, that you have yet to become aware of, but as you grow, so you will become aware of these other angels. There have always been people on Earth who are, as you say, ahead of their time, but this is done deliberately so that the information is available for you come the day you are ready to receive it. The hierarchy as you understand it is right for you, so now it is important to get to know these angels and understand them and convey this information to others."

With this information in mind I began to look at the subject with different eyes.

There are three sets of angels in each realm, heaven or choir, depending what name you care to give it, for my purpose I am calling them heavens. I now realize that they dovetail one another.

The Hierarchy

First Heaven	**Second Heaven**	**Third Heaven**
Guardian Angels	Angel Dominions	Seraphim
Archangels	Angel Powers	Ophanim
Angel Princes	Angel Virtues	Cherubim

The angels of the first heaven are the Guardian Angels, the Archangels and the Angel Princes.

The angels of the second heaven are the Angel Powers (Exousiai), the Angel Dominions (Kuriotetes) and the Angel Virtues (Dunamis).

The angels of the third heaven are the Seraphim, the Ophanim and the Cherubim.

The Third Heaven

These are the highest angels of all in human estimation. These angels create the energy of love, and they work together to send love everywhere in the universe. The third heaven is made up of the Ophanim, the Cherubim and the Seraphim.

Ophanim

The Ophanim or Angel Thrones look like wheels of fire, at least that is the only way I can describe them.

I have seen them several times. Ophanim are pure energy. I think they are the pure energy of love and that that is what they generate. When Neil H recorded *A Resonation of Angels* I saw several angel thrones that night. I did not know what they were and it was only later that I discovered what I had been seeing. When I read about them for the first time, I realized that they were exactly what I had seen. Some of the participants of the workshop also reported being covered in pillars of light when they walked on the beach after the workshop. I have seen angel thrones at workshops I've given as well, and at one in Yorkshire, one of the students could see the angel too.

Some people speculate that the angel thrones could be UFOs but having seen both, I would say most definitely not. UFOs can be circular, angel thrones are circular, but they are wheels of fire, or have been in my experience.

The Cherubim

The Cherubim are not the little cherubs that one sees in paintings, they are very strange angels indeed. They are supposed to have four faces, some of which may be animal. So they could have faces of a lion, an eagle, an ox and a man at the same time! I had thought that I had never had anything to do with the cherubim, until quite recently. I discovered that the huge animals with men's faces that were the gatekeepers to Sumerian and Assyrian cities are supposedly Cherubim. This amazed me, as many years ago I went to the British Museum to see the Egyptian artefacts they keep there. Next to the Egyptian area are these enormous pairs of statues that are from Sumer or Assyria. They are massively tall and have animal bodies with huge wings and the faces of men. They have five feet! Two when you look at them from the front and you can see four from the side, one of which is one of those that you view from the front. When I first saw them, I was awe-struck! I could not believe that people were walking past them almost as if they were not there! I found myself having to ask permission of them before I could pass between them. To me they were very sacred indeed. There are three pairs of these in the British Museum, and one pair appeared to me to be even more sacred than the others. I did not spend any more time in the Egyptian area, I could only gaze at these statues that are believed to be Cherubim. I knew in my heart that they guarded the gates. The friend I was with did not share my enthusiasm, but I returned a week later with another friend who found that she too felt the same way as myself. If ever I go to the British Museum, I have to go and visit them, they are like old friends!

A couple of years later, when I was visiting Glastonbury, I decided on a whim to go for a session of regression. I was just interested to experience it. Imagine my surprise, when I found myself outside the city of Ur and to get in I had to say the right password to these enormous gatekeepers.

The Cherubim are reputed to be the guardians of paradise and are also described as being guardians of the throne in the Holy of Holies in the temple of Solomon. They are described as being 15ft high with wings and bodies of animals with sphinx-like faces.

Ezekiel's description of them gives the impression that they are working in conjunction with the angel thrones, and that they are even carried by them. I think that in each heaven all three choirs of angels that make up that heaven work together.

The Seraphim

The last and highest form of angels is the Seraphim. These angels are the purest forms of love, which they generate by singing praises to God continually. They are reputed to perpetually sing," Holy, Holy, Holy is the Lord God and the Earth is full of his glory." This is a form of chanting, and if you have ever chanted for some considerable time, you will appreciate the power that it builds.

A few years ago, I had the opportunity to go out to Sinai with two friends to swim with a wild dolphin named Olin, who at that time would swim off the coast with some members of a Bedouin tribe who lived there. I had to learn to snorkel and find the courage to swim out of my depth, something I had never done. Olin would encourage my friend and I, by coming to within 3 feet of us and then turning and swimming out into the deeper water. Eventually I overcame my fears and happily swam out of my depth. One night as the sun was setting, the leader of our small group suggested we stood on the shoreline and chant and sing to the dolphin. I noticed that some of the Bedouins whispered amongst themselves and one of them set off at a run. My friends and I stood on the shore and we began to chant "OM" at first. The dolphin was swimming up and down just offshore and as we started to chant I noticed a difference in her behaviour. After a while she came up out of the water and stood on her tail, she then bowed very gravely to us and flipped back over into the sea. It was a truly humbling, awesome moment, she was acknowledging what we were doing. We then broke out into song. We sang 'Lord of the Dance' and as we did, I looked back at the Bedouins to see many of them had gathered to watch. They obviously knew that she loved and appreciated singing and had collected together to watch her reaction.

So I have a good understanding about how powerful chanting is, and so I realize how important the Seraphim are and how what they do is of amazing value. Many people would say that their job seems boring, but having stood within the power of Raphael (see chapter on Raphael) I know how wonderful it must be.

The angels from the very first instructed me that I must sing and chant during my workshops and at first I found that difficult, but now I love it. The angels also gave me several chants that I have included in each chapter on the archangels. It certainly helps to build up the energy, and so enables us to get closer to the angels!

So to me it would seem that the Seraphim actually fuel all the other angels with this pure divine love that they create. If we could learn to tune into the Seraphim what a difference it would make to our planet.

The Angels of the Second Heaven

The second realm is made up of the Angel Powers or Exousiai, the Angel Virtues or Dunamis and the Angel Dominions or Kuriotetes. These three sets of angels work together, to help bring peace on Earth and throughout the universe. This would appear to be a monumental task but these angels never give up on us and do their best to encourage us to become at peace with ourselves, so that peace may come to Earth.

The Angel Virtues (Dunamis)

The Angel Virtues or Dunamis as they are called in Greek, do their best to encourage our good points, they work with our conscience. When we are considering doing something that is not right for us and we get that sinking feeling, this is when these angels are doing their best to influence our consciences. Sometimes we listen sometimes we do not! The Angel Virtues work with us mainly at night in our dreams and it is during this time that our conscience listens to them. It is as if these angels recharge our consciences, but even then we may ignore it as we have free will.

They also give us self-confidence as they whisper to us in our dreams, helping us to understand that if we believe in ourselves, we are capable of so much more. They urge us to do the right thing and help create miracles in our lives and bring magic to it. They convince us through our dreams that what we wish to manifest is possible. However many of us still have doubts, and so we block our access to the miraculous side of ourselves.

They are known as the shining ones and apparently look like most people's idea of an angel, the shining white light with wings and eyes of incredible gentleness. They do their best to teach us to love freedom and to remain steadfast in the beliefs that ring true for us. They never judge us and are always encouraging us to become greater than we perceive ourselves to be.

The Dunamis are a source of comfort in times of trouble and help us deal with obstacles that bar our true path. Whenever we give of ourselves selflessly, we give energy to these angels, for they give themselves to us selflessly.

If we start to believe we can do something, these angels encourage us, and somewhere inside us if we listen, we can hear that still small voice encouraging us to continue.

I went through this experience when I was working as a receptionist. I desperately wanted to get back to the work I was trained in which was Beauty Therapy. I wanted to have my own Beauty Salon and do the work I loved, but I did not even have enough money to buy a massage couch to work on! Every time I went to work I had this tremendous feeling that I should not be there. Eventually I chanced on a scheme that would give me support whilst my business was building up, but I still did not have the money to buy a couch. However, I became convinced that I was doing the right thing for me and that somehow it would all come together.

One day there was a knock at my door and there stood a very apologetic man with a torn open letter in his hand. He explained that he lived in the house that I had previously resided in, and that he had presumed that the letter he was holding was junk mail and had given it to his small daughter to draw on! She had torn it open and he had noticed it was a cheque for me. It was a tax rebate that had been sent to the wrong address. It was just enough to buy my massage couch.

Now when I look back at that time of my life I realize just how much spiritual support and help I received, so I am very grateful to the Angel Virtues.

Angel Dominions (Kuriotetes)

The Angel Dominions or Kuriotetes – the Greek word for Dominions – are channels of mercy, light and sensitivity. They help us reconcile our differences and forgive others and ourselves. Resentment that is not released and guilt that is not forgiven are two very destructive forces. So these angels bring wisdom and understanding.

The Dominions are always on our side and can definitely see both sides of the argument. They do not judge and they plead for us whatever we may have done. They ask for mercy and forgiveness for everyone, and give only love and understanding and bring us to greater wisdom.

They see us as astonishingly beautiful entities, because they see us as our souls. I had the great fortune to see someone's soul once. I was giving a massage to a man I knew fairly well when the room was filled with a light that emanated from him. It felt different from seeing an aura and had a wonderful comforting feel. He asked what was happening as he felt he had expanded and I realized that I was seeing and feeling his soul. It is very difficult to describe, because although I could see light, it was an actual feeling as well. It was very beautiful and I was awe-struck. It totally changed my perception of him and I can never speak against him nor can I allow others to do so. When we have seen the true beauty of someone's soul it makes us realize that all of us are truly wonderful beings and that all that is wrong with people is a lack of love, and a lack of the understanding that God truly loves us all. It is our own doubts and our own perception of ourselves that get in the way. The doubts that we hold obscure us from seeing what we are truly like, and a lot of us tend to listen to the more negative opinions that people hold of us. When someone gives us a compliment instead of just saying thank you, we tend to dismiss it airily and think to ourselves that the person is just saying it to be nice!

The Angel Dominions however, have sight of us as we truly are and so are able to defend us with love and truth. These angels believe in us as we battle against negative energies that are mostly misconceptions held by ourselves. Remember when man believed that if he travelled at more than 30mph he would die! Whatever we believe comes true for us, if we believe it totally in our own hearts. If we hold any doubt we usually fail.

The Dominions are angels that do their best to bring true justice to the world, but because we are human and have free will, they do not always succeed, perhaps we need to tune in and listen more carefully to the message they send us.

The Angel Powers (Exousiai)

The Angel Powers or Exousiai – the Greek word for authority – do their best to keep the peace and to bring peace to Earth. They are also the protectors of our souls and are often seen in visions and dreams. They do their best to create peace in our souls, and the reason they do this is so that peace will be reflected on Earth and thus through the universe. Remember the saying 'As above so below'. If we can get our own souls in balance, then the Earth will follow. As Earth comes into balance, so it is easier for us to become balanced.

My mother always talked of the powers. She would say something like:

"It depends on the powers that be, if they decide that it is not right, then it will not happen."

For some reason, as a child I always just accepted this, I never thought to question her, or ask her who the powers were. I'm not even sure that she would have been able to explain. I am sure that it came from a deep resonance within her, and that this was something passed down through our family. I know that I believed her implicitly, and found myself doing the same thing as I grew older. I realize now that I have a great respect for the powers. I know that some people call the government 'the powers that be', but this was not what my mother meant, she always spoke of her 'powers' with respect and a kind of awe.

These angels are only answerable to God, but they do not act unless we ask them to intervene. So it is down to us to ask them. As there are always two sides to any problem the Powers will call upon the Angel Dominions and the Angel Virtues to help them decide which move is best to make for the good of everyone in the situation.

As they see our souls more clearly than we do, they have a much clearer picture of what is happening but I do not think I would like their task as it must be terribly difficult at times. Imagine the difficulty in dealing with someone like Saddam Hussein if the Powers received requests from humans to do so. It is then that the three choirs of angels the Powers, the Dominions and the Virtues work together. The Dominions would plead his case (remember they plead for everyone no matter what they have done) and the Virtues would support him in any way they could. However these angels cannot lie, so hopefully that makes their task easier! The Powers have to come to an understanding with the Virtues and Dominions of the truth of the matter. They are then empowered to act and they act only in the best interests of peace.

I have seen what I believe to be them, act once in my life many years ago when I lived in Malta. My children were very young then and one afternoon when they were having their afternoon nap, I was idling on the children's swing outside in a half meditative state.

Suddenly I heard a sound and I looked up into the sky. I could see many spirits coming towards me and they constantly repeated something. I cannot describe these spirits except to say they were energy and I was aware that there were many of them. As they drew closer, which took no time at all as they were moving very quickly, I could hear what they were saying. They were chanting "Nasser must die! Nasser must die!" over and over again. I was astonished! Nasser was the political leader of Egypt and the president of the United Arab Republic. He was much loved by his people and a hero in their eyes, but he was not so popular with the Western Powers. There had been much upheaval between the Egyptians and the Israelis and the British and French had intervened at times, rightly or wrongly.

I watched these spirits until they were out of sight and then I walked into the house and said to my husband, "Nasser will die tonight."

He looked at me strangely, as if thinking that I was having one of my 'funny' turns, but he was even more incredulous in the morning, when we heard on the radio that Nasser had died that night.

At the time I had no idea that these beings could be Angel Powers for I had never even heard of them. It was only later when my knowledge grew that I understood what I had seen and heard that day.

I have no idea either why the Angel Powers thought it necessary to intervene, or whether they were acting in their role as the angels of death and were there to facilitate his transition through death. I have often turned this strange experience over in my mind but have never reached a satisfactory conclusion. I leave you to make your own conclusion.

The Angel Powers are known as the angels of birth and death. These angels bring souls across and are there at death to help guide the soul to its resting place. When a relative died some years ago, I saw the angel (an Exousiai) come for him. The old man had been deaf for most of his life and had gone blind in his last few years. I remember my relative's spirit hanging there in mid air confused, and the angel flew close to him, suddenly the old man said "I can see!" and then he added, "I can hear!"

"Yes!" exclaimed the angel "You are no longer bound by earthly limitations." Then he enfolded the old man's spirit and flew away with him.

These then are the Angel Powers and these with the Angel Dominions and the Angel Virtues complete the Second Heaven.

The Angels of the First Heaven

The angels of the first heaven are the Guardian angels, the Archangels and the Angel princes. These angels work closely with humankind and are the closest set of angels to us.

Guardian Angels

Guardian angels are the angels that are closest to humans, we all have a guardian angel and some of us have more than one. Sometimes they are the spirits of loved ones who were close to us in life, so they can be someone from our family or a friend who has died, but who still has an interest in our welfare.

As we become more aware and more spiritual we may gain another guardian angel who has more knowledge than perhaps our previous angel, who nevertheless may stay with us if that helps us. Often family members can be limited by the amount of information they gathered whilst here on Earth.

Their role is to help and protect us from harm and to guide us to a better way of living. They are often hampered by the fact that we do not listen, even though they do their best to make us hear them. This can be because we do not believe in them or we think we cannot possibly be hearing the voice of our guardian angel. Our own doubts set up barriers. If we can bring ourselves to ask for help and then expect it, it more often than not arrives.

Guardian angels can also appear as humans. You can find countless stories of people who have been rescued by someone who has strangely disappeared when the person goes to look for them, or turns back to thank them. Sometimes the angel appears in angelic form, sometimes you cannot see them but you know some strong comforting force is there. Sometimes you only hear them.

When I was young I was very fond of horseriding, and I used to go to the stables to ride every Sunday. When I was fifteen, I was very slight and so was often asked to ride the ponies. One day I turned up to find the stables had purchased a new pony. Her name was Flash and she was a New Forest pony who was quite plump (in fact they weren't sure if she was pregnant) and had the most beautiful Arab head. They asked me to ride her and we set off across the fields to a large field where we circled our instructress, and moved at varying paces depending on what our teacher asked of us. I, at last, came to the front of the group and she asked me to trot on and join the other riders. I set off, but suddenly a voice spoke in my ear. It said, "You are so tired, you want to lie down on the mane." The voice repeated this several times until I felt I had to do this and I leant forward and laid my head on the mane. As my head touched the mane, I came back to this reality. I sat up to hear my instructress say, "That was very good to stay on through that!" I had no idea what had happened, so when I reached the other riders, I sidled up to the nearest and asked what had taken place. This rider informed me that Flash had gone berserk and had bucked and kicked out! He also remarked that he did not know how I had stayed on. The strange thing about this experience was that Flash seemed to have sensed it too, it made her quite overexcited and she bolted with me about five minutes later! I stayed on however and it seemed to create a bond between us. I rode her frequently after that, and I could persuade her to do things that no one else could, and the only rosette I ever won was riding Flash.

Another example of a guardian angel happened to a friend of mine whose daughter was physically attacked. My friend went to intervene and as she did she asked the angels for help. She said she could physically feel an entity between her and the attacker. After it was over, my friend found her only injury was her broken glasses! Her daughter said that she had seen the attacker bite her, and they inspected her arms, and there were no bite marks and my friend never felt a thing.

So you see that guardian angels can and do many things. These are the angels that many people see and experience and if you would like to meet up with yours, then I will tell you how to go about it in the next chapter!

The Archangels

The next highest angels in the hierarchy are the archangels, which is what this book is principally about. I have been working with the archangels for many years and many people have asked for the information I have given them in workshops to be written down in the form of a book. So here it is!

There are many archangels, but I have chosen to write about the seven that are the most commonly known and accepted.

The archangels are concerned mostly with our spiritual growth and each archangel it is believed has legions of angels that work with him in his name. The archangels each represent an aspect of love, so that together they are love in every facet. Together it would seem, that they form an enormous faceted diamond, that shines forth rainbows in every direction. That of course would be if we could look at the archangels from a distance! It is the archangels that bring the important messages, such as Gabriel when he visited Mary, to give news of Jesus' birth.

Each archangel works on a particular colour ray. The seven archangels I am dealing with represent the higher octave of colour. This is the octave that stands above our visible rainbow, and this second rainbow is coloured white, violet, ruby-gold, pink, electric blue, emerald green and golden yellow. As I said earlier, they also represent a facet of love; thus Zadkiel stands for mercy and forgiveness and Jophiel for wisdom. Wisdom may not appear to you to be a facet of love, however to become wise you have usually learnt a lot about love and life, and wisdom is a lot about learning to love unconditionally.

The Angel Princes

The angel princes or principalities are the other angels that make up the first heaven and these angels take care of nations, regions and countries. I find that they too have legions of angels working for them. When I have worked with them, there appear to be many angels that assist them. The angel princes are the angels we need to contact when we are doing our best to improve our surroundings. They give protection when asked and do their best to protect the fabric of the Earth. These angels are very large indeed. One of my friends, whose daughter frequently sees them, told her mother one day that one was present. My friend asked to be shown where the angel was. The young girl replied that you could only see his foot, as they were so large! However those angels that give assistance to the angel princes appear to be much smaller.

These angels do not seem to be recognized as much as the archangels and the guardians, so it is good to make the effort to have contact with them. When your country or countryside is threatened in some way these are the angels to ask for help.

I live in Cornwall and we Cornish feel that Cornwall is a country and not just a county in England. We therefore have our own angel prince and his attendant angels. When Devon (the county next to Cornwall) had many cases of foot and mouth disease in their cattle, I and some others asked the angel prince to keep the disease out of Cornwall and to keep our cattle safe. I would ask this of him every day, during the epidemic. The disease did get into Cornwall but only about a mile over the border. It never got any further. This was despite lorries from Devon bringing carcasses into Cornwall to bury on our land. People would say to me that Cornwall could not possibly escape from getting it, but a few others and I kept asking the angel prince to help and spread love throughout our land. Some of you will say that you could just as easily pray to God, and this is so. However these angels are working specifically with the land, so it does not hurt to ask. As my father used to say, "If you never ask, you never get!" These angels as are all angels, are answerable to God anyway.

I tell you this story, only to make you think. You can do this too! Whenever we have a crisis if we ask and send love to the angel in charge, it helps him/her to overcome many problems. After all if we do not let our angel know what we want, how can he/she ever give it to us?

These three sets of angels make up the first realm or heaven.

This then finishes the hierarchy, we have travelled through the third heaven of the Ophanim (Thrones), the Cherubim and the Seraphim. Then on through the second heaven of the Exousiai (Powers), The Kuriotetes (Dominions) and the Dunamis (Virtues), to the first heaven of Guardian angels, the Archangels and the Angel Princes. Let us continue then to study the angels of the first heaven in more depth.

2

Guardian angels

Guardian angels work very closely with human beings. Each of us has a guardian angel and they do their very best to help us. They work hard to warn us of dangers and show us the best way forward and reflect the voice of our hearts.

Unfortunately, we don't always listen or notice. It takes time and patience to really listen and often it then takes great courage and trust to follow what we hear, see or feel. Trust is something that we have to build between the angels and ourselves. When we first make contact with our guardian angel it is a joyous moment, but after a while, unless we make the effort to stay in contact we can begin to doubt what we feel and ourselves.

Often I meet people who say something like "I'm told that I have a guardian angel called Miriam and she watches over me all the time!" That is fine if we choose to do nothing about it, and just bask in that knowledge, but if we apply ourselves a little more, we can have a much more rewarding relationship with our guardian angel.

Guardian angels are there to help us to live our lives in a better manner and solve problems. They help to keep our lives on an even keel, and support us through troubled times. In fact, they often keep trouble away from us. When we learn to read the signs they offer, then we can avoid problem situations. I have been guided to shops that I never knew existed, and shown books I needed to read. I have also been warned not to take a certain route when driving and so avoided a bad accident.

They can also reassure you when you begin to doubt yourself. A few years ago, I began to doubt that I was doing the right thing. I wondered if I was getting above myself and if I ought to leave this kind of work to others who in my eyes were probably better qualified. So I asked for a sign to show me if I was on the right path. I asked for coloured feathers, as I thought this could be possible but was not so easy as white ones. As I live in a seaside town, the place tends to be littered with white seagull feathers! When you make such a request, you tend to forget that you've done it as you continue with the daily round of your life. Which I did!

On my day off, my husband and I decided we would go for a walk on Bodmin Moor. We chose one of the popular circular walks and set off from St Breward, downwards on a path lined by trees, into the valley. We had not been walking long when I noticed that the birdsong around us sounded strangely different to the usual sounds we hear. I remarked on this to my husband who agreed. We decided that they sounded like tropical birds! We rounded a corner and there in front of us was a tropical bird farm! Intrigued, we went inside, and I asked the gentleman behind the counter if they sold feathers. He told me that they did not, but I was welcome to help myself to any I found. Well! I had red ones, green ones, blue ones, yellow ones, and some of variegated colours. In fact so many that I shouted mentally to the heavens "Okay! I get the message!" I laughed a lot on my walk that day and I kept all the feathers and made a display of them to remind me whenever the doubts creep in!

This is one of the things that guardian angels help with and when you first get in contact with yours, you need to assure yourself that it is really your guardian angel. So you need to ask for a sign or something that is proof to you. Many people ask for feathers as I did, but it needs to be something that you think is possible but not so likely. Often when you are on this kind of path, it is difficult to convince sceptics, as many of the messages we have received are heard, seen or felt only by ourselves and we are dealing with the unseen. Therefore it is important that the sign you choose is something that only you and your angel understand. While you are waiting, you may tell others, if you wish, what that sign is, because that will add confirmation. It is also helpful if you write down your experiences and date them, as you will find that when you read them later you may have forgotten some of the details.

You can ask your angel for whatever you feel appropriate, but if it is a question, often it needs to be phrased in such a way as to make the answer a definite yes or no. I have asked for all sorts of things over the years. Even when I was a child and really did not understand about angels, I asked God for the sound of a stone hitting a tin, to let me know what time my grandmother died. My father had told me that evening that she was dying.

In the morning I was able to tell my father and brother the time she died, before they could tell me. This may seem odd, but it was very important to me at the time.

Rainbows are always signs to me that that everything is going the right way. My mother always told me that the first thing she saw in the sky after I was born was a rainbow. When my eldest daughter was born, I rang my mother to tell her, and she told me that she already knew because a rainbow had appeared over the house where we lived. This continued with my second daughter, who was born in Malta, and a rainbow appeared over the island, as I looked down on it from the maternity hospital.

You can be quite inventive about the signs you choose for your communications with the angels. The more you trust your angel the greater your ability to tune in and receive messages, the greater your confidence becomes.

Asking the angels for help is important. As soon as you ask you set up a line of contact which enables them to come closer to you and help you. This is really very important; ask, ask, ask! Your guardian angel is your first port of call; he or she is waiting for contact and waiting for the chance to help you. Sometimes your guardian angel can be someone who was close to you earlier in your life, such as a grandmother or grandfather. As you grow in knowledge, so you may receive information from higher sources, but your original guardian angel stays with you. Mine is named Daniel and I did not know him in life, or at least not in this one! He helps me with many things and a lot of the smaller things I would rather nor ask the archangels about! Daniel helps me get out of side turnings on to busy roads safely and sometimes to find parking spots if I'm going to a busy town. In fact he helps me with all sorts of things; he will help me with my clients and some of their problems.

It is often these smaller things that strengthen our belief, and as you work more and more with them, you gain even greater access and ask for help with even bigger problems.

My daughter was living in an old run-down cottage which was damp and I was worried about my grandsons' health. One night I asked the angels for help to find her a better place to live. A couple of days later, she rang to tell me that her landlord had given her notice to get out as he wished to sell the property. I was horrified! Then I realized that the angels must have been finding her somewhere better to live. Sure enough before the month was out, a better place to live that was warm and dry materialized!

When something like this happens to you, remember to say thank you. It is really important. At times I have kept a book, just to write thank you for all the good things that have happened to me during the day. Angels need to feel appreciated just as much we do!

No problem is too large or too small for the angels and they will help you. Once you have asked, it is necessary to let them get on with it and for you to trust and know that it will come about. I find that it is better not to try and visualize how it could happen, just let it unfold naturally. The angels have far better imagination than we have, and often find ways that we would never have even dreamed about. In fact, on reflection, I don't think that you have to even believe that it will happen, you just have to ask.

A few years ago a lady came to me at a show in Totnes for a palmistry reading. I looked at her palms and apparently said, "You're ill aren't you?"

She had replied "Yes. It's the smoking. I've smoked for 45 years and I've been trying to give it up for 40!"

I told her that she should ask her angels for help. She looked at me sceptically and so I added, "Well, what harm can it do you?"

After the reading, she told me later that she wandered amongst the stalls, thinking about what I had told her. To her surprise she found she had come to rest by an angel stall. She treated herself to some angel cards and drew one, to find it told her to stop abusing her body and take more care of herself! Taking this as a sign, she decided to ask as she felt it would do no harm. Over a year later, she came on one of my angel courses. She told me that nothing had ever been so easy, the smoking had just left her and she hadn't smoked for about 9 months!

I have just spoken to the lady in question to ask her permission to tell her story and she told me that she had never smoked since. She also told me that she had been asking her angels for speakers to come to her newly formed awareness group, she wanted to ask me, but felt she didn't like to bother me! Then here was I phoning her! Angels are simply amazing!

Laughter helps the angels to get closer to us. Although the angels can work with us when we are sad, it is not so easy. When we are laughing, our auras are large and positive, when we are sad we draw our aura around us like a man in a coat in the wind. Remember the old story about the wind and the sun having a competition to see who could get the old man to take off his coat first? The wind blew and blew, but the old man clutched his coat more tightly around him and just wouldn't let go. Then came the sun's turn and the sun just shone on the old man, who eventually became so hot that he took his coat off. Our auras work in the same way, they are large when we are happy and small when we are sad. When you laugh with the angels they bathe in your warmth. When you cry they feel shut out, so they do their best to comfort you with their own warmth.

When you are positive you draw positive experiences to you, when you are negative you draw negative experiences. Try it for yourself. When you get up in the morning and you feel good, notice how your day will stay that way. If you get up angry and fed up, you can bet your life that you will spill the milk or fall over the cat and things start to go wrong. Next time you wake up feeling out of sorts and at odds with the world, take time to quieten yourself and ask the angels for help. Tell yourself that it is going to be a good day and refuse to let negativity take over.

I am no different to the rest of the human race, I have problems, doubts and fears, but my advantage is that I work with the angels. I trust them and they have never disappointed me. Sometimes when I listen to my clients' worries I feel I am very lucky, because I can see a path that is so much easier. All it takes is trust and the courage to ask. So bear this in mind when you are communing with the angels.

How do you contact the angels? There are several methods of approach. One of the best ways is through meditation or going into the silence. This takes patience and determination. It means sitting down in a quiet room on a hard chair for at least 20 minutes a day.

Before you begin, ask for the protection of one of the archangels. Say something along the lines of, "Archangel Michael, please protect me with your cloak of blue throughout my meditation. I feel it forming around me as I speak and I thank you for this."

Then concentrate on breathing slowly and deeply, and work on making your body relax. Make sure your feet are flat on the floor and that you have not crossed your arms or legs. Imagine your body as being very heavy and feel yourself relax and wherever you find tension, tell your body to relax and let go of the tension. Doing this just for relaxation's sake will be very beneficial to you. Then work on emptying your mind of all thought. This is the tricky bit, as your ego will start to come up with things like "Did you remember to lock the car?" In fact, anything that will divert your attention from your purpose. The ego gets frightened that it will have nothing to do if you master this art of meditation, so it keeps trying to catch your attention and divert it. Often it will succeed! Do your best not to be put off by this, just bring your attention gently back to the task in hand.

I find it helps to imagine a blank white wall in front of you and fix your attention upon it. Every time you find your mind wandering, bring its focus back to the wall. Gradually over time pictures will form on the wall, and at first you may find it produces colours and patterns that change, a bit like a child's kaleidoscope. When you experience this you know you are getting there! Sometimes you may feel sensations like cobwebs being drawn over your face. Just stay alert, watch, listen and feel. This is why you use a hard chair. It stops you from falling asleep, and if you stay totally relaxed, your mind will start to tune in to a higher vibratory wavelength. This is the wavelength of the angels.

At first you will probably find that nothing happens and this is the point where you have to find the courage to continue until you feel, hear or see something. The moment you sense someone near you, ask questions.

1. Who are you?
2. What is your name?
3. Why are you here?
4. What do you want of me?

Listen and feel within your body to any answers. Do they feel truthful? If it doesn't feel right, repeat the question three times. It is a universal law with spirit that truth has to be told on the third asking. Very occasionally you can make contact with a spirit that is not angelic and that is why it is so important to ask for protection from an archangel before you begin. There are some spirits that are just playful and like leading you up the garden path. Often they will tell you, what they think you want to hear. It is easy for them because in that realm they have clairvoyance and clairaudience, so they can easily pick up things from you. That is why, and I say it again, it is important to ask for the protection of one of the archangels.

Do not despair if nothing happens. It was the same for me when I first started. I was attending a class and we were all working to get contact with a guide or guardian angel, to help us work in greater depth. Everyone else seemed to be succeeding but me! However, I kept on going and one day I did get what looked like an arch-bishop in purple robes smiling at me and then he was gone! I received nothing more. I became very frustrated! Others were describing their experiences, conversations etc. and I still had zilch!

My teacher sympathised with me and said that maybe I needed to agree to serve. Then I remembered that I had had contact with spirit on and off throughout my whole life. Once I had reached adulthood, spirit had come to me often and asked me to serve. I wasn't sure what they meant, but I wasn't keen on the idea. It felt to me that I would become their pawn and would have to follow their instructions to the letter. So my answer had always been an emphatic "No way!" At times I know they despaired of me and I can still feel a twinge of guilt about it!

However around the time that I was trying to make contact, I was meeting up with another group of individuals from all over Cornwall. We would discuss subjects in depth, and one day we talked about service.

As we talked about it I came to realize that I would be helping and that my individuality would not be lost. I walked out of that meeting feeling totally different. As I drove home, I kept shouting at the skies, "I will serve! I will serve! Okay!"

The next morning I sat down to meditate and I asked that my guide would come through. Immediately I had contact!

So if you are having difficulties at first, be patient and then consider that perhaps you need to agree to serve. Does this path feel right to you? We are all unique and for some it is right and for others it is not. Even if you cannot make contact with your guardian angel, he or she is still there and you can still ask for help and for signs.

The following guided meditation is another way of making contact, which you may choose to use. You will need to read it through and then either ask someone to read it to you while you go into meditation or record it on a cassette tape. Play the tape and listen and follow it after carrying out the following actions.

1. Find a peaceful place.
2. Put some oils of your choice on an oil burner.
3. Light a candle.
4. Sing some songs you like, or play some music and dance to it.
5. Drink some water or fruit juice laced with Guardian angel essence .
6. Ask Michael for protection during the meditation.

Now sit down and relax and breathe deeply, turn on the tape and listen to it. Do not worry if you lose parts of it, it just means you went deeper at that point. You will always hear the relevant points for you.

Here is the guided meditation. Where you find ......
it means pause for a while. When you record it yourself, remember to put in the pauses, you will need them when you come to follow it.

Meeting your Guardian Angel

Take a deep breath and allow your body to relax, let your feet feel heavy to the point that you could not move them if you wanted to, let this feeling travel up through your calves into your thighs so that your legs feel very heavy...... Then let this feeling travel up through your body...... Continue to breathe very deeply and let the feeling travel into your arms and hands. Your whole body feels very relaxed now. You take another deep breath and let this relaxed feeling travel into your head, your jaw and your eyes...... You now feel very relaxed, very safe and comfortable.

Breathing in deeply, imagine a long white spiral staircase forming in the middle of the room, as you look up at it you see angels hovering around it, although the staircase looks a little transparent, you notice that the steps seem very solid. You see an angel beckoning to you, and pointing to the staircase and knowing in your mind, that you are perfectly safe and that the angels will guard you, you start walking towards the steps and with the encouragement of the angels you begin the climb up the stairs. Feel the steps underneath your feet and have a sense of moving upwards, as you get higher you can look back down and see the building you have left your body in below you...... This view is much the way you would see it from an aircraft.

You keep on climbing.

Suddenly you come out through a silvery mist, on to a beautiful plateau. The first thing you notice is the perfume, the smell of the roses, the lilacs, the orange trees and the freesias. You see all of these plants growing around a path that disappears into the distance. You can hear birds singing and you are aware that the crystals on the sides of the path are resonating with a beautiful sound. There are amethysts, quartz, citrines, sapphires, emeralds and rubies. Each emanates a beautiful soft sound.

You start to walk along the path watching the butterflies as they fly in front of you, look at their wonderful colourful wings, some are almost transparent and translucent. The birdsong you hear as you walk along fills your heart with joy. The sun is shining brightly and you can feel the heat on your back as you gaze at this place in wonder. You have never felt so safe and so at peace.

As you follow the pathway you hear the splash of water and notice a small waterfall running into a deep pool that has water lilies growing on it. You walk around the edge of the pool listening to the water as it flows into the pool. You feel safe, protected and at peace. You pause a while and absorb the peace of this exquisite place......

You trail your hand through the water and feel its coolness on your skin. It is refreshing and so you cup your hands together and bring some water to your lips and sip it from your hands. You feel the water cool in your mouth and your throat and realize that it has a healing energy that spreads throughout your body making you feel stronger, more whole and complete.

Renewed, you continue along the path until it widens to reveal a large fountain, you gaze at the fountain for a while until you realize that there is a warmth coming off it, and you understand that this is a fountain of shining white light...... You move closer so that its rays pour down over you filling you with joy and happiness dissolving all fear and apprehension. You feel energized and confident, confident that you are going to meet your own guardian angel.

Now, you can hear angels singing, the sound is very comforting and you move towards it. There on either side of the path stand rows of angels, they beckon to you, and they are laughing and singing and as you walk between them. You hear one speak, saying, "I bless you with joy!" and another says "I bless you with laughter!" and another, "I bless you with love!" As you pass, each angel blesses you. You are blessed with good health, wealth, happiness, beauty, and peace, serenity, confidence, strength and much more. Just listen!

As you reach the end of the row, you see the path stretching onwards and you see steps leading up to what appears to be an amazing temple. Its beauty holds you spellbound...... You gaze at the amazing architecture and the colours of the walls. ...... make a mental note of this information. You see a door and by the door stands an angel of incredible light and beauty. You walk towards this angel and as you approach, the angel turns to you and says, "I am your guardian angel. I have done my best to help you in every way, but now if you will step within these walls, together we can build a friendship, so that I may support you in everything you do. I can give you encouragement when you feel low, and laugh with you when all goes well. This building that we walk into now, represents you. Notice its splendor, for in truth you are a divine being who has forgotten how wonderful you are."

As you walk into the temple take note of the colours and the architecture, remember that what you see and hear and feel are all part of you, and remember to ask for the name of your guardian angel. I will leave you now for a while to talk with your guardian angel and to gaze at the wonder that you truly are. After a while I will call you back......

I am calling you back now; let your guardian angel come with you as you retrace your steps, out of your temple and back along the path past the angels of blessings, who sing farewells to you...... Feel the warmth as you pass by the fountain of light and contemplate the beauty of the water lilies as you continue on by the pool and waterfall......

Walk on through the trees and flowers with the bees busily buzzing around them, smell the perfume of the

44

flowers and again feel the heat of the sun shining on you, as you move along the path.

At last you come to the spiral staircase. You walk down confidently knowing that you are supported and protected. As you look down you can see angels floating below you and you can see the building that you left earlier. Slowly you descend, and at last you are walking across the room and back into your body. Let your senses adjust and become familiar within your body again. Feel the surface below you, and hear any noises around you, and when you are ready open your eyes, take a deep breath and look round.

After you have returned and settled from your meditation, settle yourself down and write down what happened for you in your meditation. If you feel you did not make contact, then do the meditation again another time.

Remember to take note of the gifts you were blessed with and also that the building you saw was you. What did you notice about it and can you match this up with yourself? Were you blown away by what you saw and felt? If so, than its time to reappraise yourself, and accept yourself as you truly are.

Once you have made contact with your guardian angel then you can start to work with him/her. Meditate as often as you can and build a relationship; it will be one that you will always be grateful for. When you decide you are ready to work with the archangels, remember to call in your guardian angel to help you with this.

3

Archangel Gabriel

Gabriel, glowing giant of gladness,
Grace us with your glorious spirit,
Come to us when life has sadness,
Fill us with your gentle mirth.

Gabriel uses the white ray of purity to bring through his amazing transformational energy. White is the higher octave of red and stands for cosmic purity. We need to remember that white contains all the colours and therefore contains the rainbow. The rainbow has always been seen as a bridge between the spirit and physical worlds and this is why it is associated with Gabriel. Every soul, it is believed, has been touched by the energy of Gabriel, as it is he that brings every soul across from spirit to birth. Indeed, it is said in the bible that Gabriel brought the news to Mary of Jesus' impending birth. He is also reputed to have dictated the Koran to Mohammed. His spiritual home is believed to be between Sacramento and Mount Shasta, California.

Gabriel has a lot to do with children; he says we need to constantly look at life through the eyes of a child, seeing the wonder and versatility of life as if for the first time. His energy has that wonderful childlike quality and exuberance that I see in my youngest grandson. Recently my grandson was walking on the beach with me when he became incredibly excited, and started pointing at something. He eagerly ran across the beach to a wall where a piece of green moss was growing. He thought it was just wonderful. I would never have noticed it if Jay had not pointed it out to me! This is the kind of attitude Gabriel wishes to promote in us, to be truly awake and observant all of the time.

I had always thought that as Gabriel stood for purity, he would be rather strict and meticulous. I am ashamed to say that I thought he might be 'holier than thou.' I first met him when he came to help a client on whom I was working; and I will never be able to forget that wonderful energy. Even as I think of it now, it brings a glow to my heart. He is full of laughter, joy, happiness, love, exuberance and an intense feeling of being held by someone that laughs at trouble and can always make one smile. He does not know sadness as we know it, he only feels compassion for us when we cannot feel and appreciate his intense joy of life. He loves nothing more than for us to find his passion for joy and innocence.

Gabriel cleanses us and helps us to return to our innocent, pure life-stream of energy that flows through the universe experiencing joy wherever it touches or moves. It dances to the pure unadulterated rhythm of life and its sound expresses clear delight. It is that feeling when someone does something for you that is an unexpected wonderful surprise! Life could be so much happier and full of wonder if we were to make the effort to touch into Gabriel's energy at the beginning of every day. Touch into it and let Gabriel light your day!

My daughter started to paint Gabriel one evening, and was delighted next morning to see a rainbow. She felt this meant that Gabriel was with her. However, she was to see a rainbow every day until she had finished the painting! When you work with his energy, you need to be ready for gentle jokes, in fact anything that makes you smile! You will find that your purest essence emerges and that essence is joyful love.

You hear the expression on television now of 'white-lighters'. These are Gabriel's legions and you may feel the need to work with this energy. If Gabriel comes and takes your hand, dance with it all for a while and enjoy the pure delight of life. Walk away from the shadows and let the sun shine on your life again.

To get in touch with this wonderful energy, find yourself a space of half an hour or longer. Start by singing all those songs you learned as a child such as 'If you're happy and you know it clap your hands!' Any song that has a joyful rhythm and expresses happiness. No sad songs for Gabriel. If you are able, do the actions with the song and dance with it! Use drums if you wish! Think back to your childhood and ask yourself, what you did for pure joy in those days. What made you laugh? What was fun for you?

If those days were dark days for you, then imagine the kind of childhood you would have liked to experience.

Then begin to live it in your mind. Gabriel is particularly caring for those whose childhoods were in shadow. It is your time to come out into the light and bask in Gabriel's sun. Put those hard times behind you and find that essence of pure joy within yourself.

Another chant you could sing is the following:

I'm wearing my long wing feathers, as I fly
I'm wearing my long wing feathers as I fly,
I circle around, I circle around,
The boundaries of the Earth.
Higher, Higher, Higher, and Higher.
Higher, Higher, Higher, and Higher.

Light four white candles, bring out quartz crystals and drink rainbow charged water containing Gabriel essence. Use some of the Gabriel oils on a burner (choose from those set out below). Play the music of Gabriel's resonation, seat yourself comfortably and stare at Gabriel's picture. Focus only on this and let yourself be filled with Gabriel's love and do your best to feel his love.

Gabriel says

Treat life as the most precious gift you will ever receive, nurture it, love it, enjoy it. Feel the laughter of new adventure, feel the joy of being able to touch everything around you, plants, animals and other humans. Let yourself explore the land of music and delight in it all. Remember to use all your senses and remember we, in spirit, are here to support you in your quest for happiness. Pursue it with every ounce of your being and laugh, laugh and laugh again, especially when everything goes wrong! Just enjoy the joke! Call me if you need me for I am always here!

Oils linked to Gabriel

ROSEMARY *(Rosemary officianalis)*
Greater Ray: White
Lesser Ray: Blue
Ruling Planet: Sun
Element: Fire
Chakras affected: Base and Throat
Precautions: Avoid in epilepsy, high blood pressure and
   pregnancy
This oil was used to drive out evil spirits and is symbolic of memory and is worn for remembrance. Rosemary helps with past life recall and improves the memory. Good for the morning blues and mind strengthening. It is initially awakening and then very relaxing. Good for meditation. Rosemary gives excellent mental clarity,

so is very good when you need to focus. This oil works on the astral body, comforting it. It is accepted as a spiritual protector.

LILY OF THE VALLEY *(Convallaria Magalis)*
Greater Ray: White
Lesser Ray: Ruby and Gold
Ruling Planet: Mercury
Element: Air
Chakras affected: Heart
Precautions: Not used in aromatherapy
Aids the memory and instils peace. It helps you recall ancient information. Lily of the Valley was always brought to me as a child, when I was ill, and I was always very appreciative of its wonderful aroma. Apollo is supposed to have presented this plant to Aesculapius. It stands for humility, renewal and spiritual awareness.

NEROLI *(Citrus aurantium / vulgaris)*
Greater Ray: White
Lesser Ray: Golden Yellow
Ruling Planet: Sun
Element: Fire
Chakras affected: Solar Plexus and Sacral
Precautions: None found
Neroli is always cheering and is often used for depres-

sion. It makes you relax and feel better about life. This oil balances you, bringing back the joy and helps you gain understanding of your problems. Neroli is truly a Gabriel oil.

4

Archangel Zadkiel

Zadkiel, angel of true mercy,
Help us forgive all those who've hurt us,
Fill us with your great compassion
And set us free for evermore.

Zadkiel uses the violet ray of mercy, compassion, freedom and forgiveness. Violet is the higher octave of orange and stands for transmutation. Zadkiel helps us to set ourselves free from guilt and resentment, which then allows us to forgive ourselves and others. In so doing we transform ourselves and lift ourselves to a higher vibration. His spiritual home is believed to be over the island of Cuba.

Violet puts us in touch with our souls or higher selves and it helps us to remember whom we truly are and why we chose to come here. It allows us to discard out-moded views and beliefs that stop us from being all that we can be. We become free. Violet allows us to think and see from world consciousness, instead of just from our own viewpoint.

Zadkiel encourages us to do this, setting us free from the chains and bonds that we allow to hold us back. He helps us to realize that it actually does more damage to hold on to resentment and past hurt. When we hold resentment against someone, it forms a chain between ourselves and the person we resent. It then becomes a tug of war between the two, as each feeds it with negative energy, because if we resent them, it is highly likely that they resent us! As soon as we let go of it, we have more energy and we feel lighter. We have, after all, cast off a burden.

Zadkiel's energy is full of compassion, he understands that sometimes we feel hurt and unloved. He soothes us with his calming energy, assuring us that we are always loved and cared for, and if we let go of the hurt, we will become more whole. We will then have more love to give and more room to receive love. Hurts attract negativity and so bring us even more pain and even more to resent. When we let go, Zadkiel then causes more positive experiences to come to us. It seems to be that when we are sorry for ourselves we create a protective barrier around ourselves that keeps out a lot of the good things that we desire. Zadkiel works tirelessly to help us remove these barriers. It appears that he and his angels fuel the violet flame that we carry, so that as we let go of the blockages, the violet flame burns the brighter. We can always choose to see life in a different manner in any moment.

Let Zadkiel help you drop the scales from your eyes. A friend who saw the painting of Zadkiel could not take her eyes away from it, even when she closed her eyes she was still seeing the painting. This remained for at least three days. I realize now that this was when Zadkiel began to work with her, supporting her through many trials and tribulations. Several years passed before she came to me to tell me that the scales had fallen from her eyes, and she could now see and understand everything more clearly.

Zadkiel has immense amounts of patience. He will feed us more and more information and send people to us who will give their support, until slowly he releases the bonds that tie us. It is amazing how inventive we can be, as we try to hold on to our petty resentments and refuse to see the bigger picture. Zadkiel of course is even more innovative and constantly finds ways to let us see and hear the truth.

I am sitting writing this on a wonderful sunny April day and the seagulls have just come screaming down over me, to remind me that they can act as messengers of Zadkiel. They represent freedom and shout at us sometimes, "Let go! Let go!" Years ago, when my first marriage broke down, I was living far inland. I wanted to leave the marriage, but felt unable to as I had two small children. One morning a seagull arrived and settled himself on a post in the garden. From that day forward he would harangue me with,

"Go home! Go home!"

I would rail at him with tears running down my face, "I can't! I don't know how!"

Things suddenly changed, and I saw a way out of my predicament. The morning I left the seagull was not there. His work was done!

When I arrived back in Cornwall however, about a hundred of them flew down over me. They shouted,

"Welcome home! At last you've seen sense! Welcome to freedom!"

So you see how Zadkiel works with us. He is truly inspiring!

I wanted a way to make it easier to bring the angelic energies through to humans and so I journeyed to the angelic realms and spoke to Zadkiel. He told me to make essences. I asked him what to use for a base. He smiled and said that I owned it already. He told me it was in the first cupboard on the left-hand side of my kitchen, at the back of the first shelf on the right! I came out of my meditation and rushed downstairs to look. There, exactly as he had said was an essence that had been given to me by a friend. She had told me that it was very special and was for me. She told me that when she had made it she had held it up to look at it and her house was struck by lightning! She swore that the lightning had gone into the essence, and that it was definitely for me to use. Thus the angelic essences were born.

To work with Zadkiel light seven violet coloured candles and have amethysts, sugilite and any other violet coloured crystals nearby. Use oils on a burner (see the list of oils that correspond to Zadkiel). Drink some violet charged water with Zadkiel essence in. Write down the names of those that you wish to forgive, or sometimes it can be a situation, and place them with the crystals. Sing or chant to raise the vibrations, it's easier for them to contact us if we raise the energy. I like to use Louise L. Hay's chant, "I forgive everyone, I forgive myself," or you can use the following:

> Zadkiel hear us softly singing,
> Fill us with your love,
> Zadkiel, help us set ourselves free,
> Fill us with your love.
>
> Zadkiel hear us softly calling,
> Fill us with your love,
> Zadkiel fill us with forgiveness,
> Fill us with your love.

You can also use singing bowls to attract the angels if you wish.

Then, sit quietly and focus on Zadkiel's picture, play his resonance from the Angel CD and ask Zadkiel to give you the knowledge you need to set you free, do your best to really feel his energy. Remember there is no blame. Afterwards, destroy the pieces of paper you have written names on, either by burning them or tearing them into small bits and flushing them down the toilet.

Zadkiel says

The more you can forgive others, the more you can forgive yourself, the lighter your physical body will be. Call on me for help and I will surround you with circumstances that will allow you to see the truth and help you find a way to let go of the pain. Treat yourself to lots of pure water to drink, and bathe yourself in hot water containing oils and sea salts. This will give you the space to throw off your burdens. Sometimes it will take a while to release the old patterns, but as you do, you will know that you have changed and you will sense my energy around you. Then go forward with renewed verve. This way, together, we treat each other with compassion and respect and allow the earth to take her proper place in the cosmos. Love yourself more, respect yourself and gain integrity.

Oils associated with Zadkiel

LAVENDER *(Lavandula Angustifolium)*
Greater Ray: Violet
Lesser Ray: Blue
Ruling planet: Mercury
Element: Air
Precautions: Avoid the oil in the early months of
   pregnancy

It has a good effect on all the chakras but particularly on the throat and spleen. Lavender's key words are Magic, Love, Protection, Healing and Vision. Reputedly contains the sacred violet fire and this is why it helps every situation. Appears to stabilize the etheric, astral and physical bodies. Lavender is said to change the way we think about love. During times when we have to make changes, it helps re-programme the mind and helps us get to deeper levels in trance channelling. It is said to calm wild lions and tigers, and I have discovered that Lavender plants are often used in zoos to do just that, and they love it! A friend of mine also used Lavender to calm a bull she owned, that had never been handled. She told me that the bull became very calm and went quite easily into the trailer, when he needed to be taken elsewhere.

AMBER *(Sucinum oleum)*
Greater Ray: Violet
Lesser Ray: Ruby Gold
Ruling planet: Uranus
Element: Air
Chakras affected: Crown, but has a clearing effect on them all
Precautions: This is a very powerful oil, so use it warily
Amber particularly helps the spleen and solar plexus

chakras. This oil is the highest note of all; it raises the vibrations bringing a new balance throughout. It clears the aura of stains from tobacco, drugs and alcohol and eases withdrawal symptoms. Amber clears the mind and makes a better channel to the angels.

V I O L E T *(Viola Odorata)*
Major Ray: Violet
Minor Ray: Emerald Green
Ruling Planet: Venus
Element: Earth
Chakras affected: Crown and Sacral
Precautions: None known
Violet in olden times was known for driving away evil spirits. I can agree with that because as a child, when I was angry, I would go and sit on the bank where the violets grew, and tell them all my troubles. I always came away happier and calmer! The oil is used to treat anger and is very calming. It is said to comfort the heart, so it is good when relationships are breaking up. Valerie Ann Worwood states that it helps us overcome timidity and helps us let our light shine through.

5

Archangel Uriel

Uriel, angel of tranquillity,
Give to us your peace of mind,
Help us see with total clarity,
Help us know the true divine.

Uriel uses the ruby gold ray of peace and tranquillity. This ray allows us to ground our wisdom and bring it into our reality. The more we know of ourselves, the greater the peace and tranquillity within us. This shines through us as serenity. Ruby gold is the higher octave of yellow and stands for the ministration of peace and the love of all nature.

Uriel uses many senses to bring through his energy. He feels that the psychic sense is the greatest and truest sense of them all. The psychic sense brings all the senses together in a culmination of truth.

Uriel elected to be blind because he says that it is easier to 'see' without physical sight. Uriel sees everything. There is nothing that we can hide from him and because of this, his touch brings a new peace, a quiet mind and a much greater awareness. As our awareness grows, so we feel much safer and more secure. We can anticipate what is coming and find easier ways of doing things. We can sense which is the safest path to take, and this may be the path that others decry, but we know in our hearts that it is the right one for us. We trust and step forward and find that we were right to trust. As we move to greater awareness, we step with even greater belief and understand when odd things happen, that it is all part of the plan to show us who we really are.

Uriel carries the candle of hope and if we look at the painting we will see the candles in the eyes behind the depiction of Uriel. He is working to bring peace to the world, and he keeps the candle of hope burning in the darkest places on Earth. He fans the flame in our hearts to urge us on to greater service to humanity.

Actually experiencing the peace that Uriel generates is a humbling thing. When he wraps his ruby gold cloak around us, the peace is immense and deafening in its calm and silence. As one client put it, "You feel that you are wrapped in a thick fur that is so safe and comforting". I have friends who have built a Saxon round house and when I walk into it, it feels like 'thick' peace. Those are the only words I can find to describe it, and the presence of Uriel is so strong, I feel I can reach out and touch it and rub it between my fingers.

Often we find Uriel in the darker spaces, carrying his special light, so that we may see. It is good sometimes to touch into his energy in caves. Here we can feel his peace surrounding us. It clears our minds and enables us to 'see' with a greater clarity.

Uriel is the angel who came to Enoch and instructed him in the study of the stars. In the book of Enoch, Uriel shows him 'the signs and the times and the years and the days'. In the book *Uriel's Machine* by Christopher Knight and Robert Lomas, they actually rebuild a device following the instructions received from Uriel by Enoch. They state that it is an extremely accurate timing device.

Uriel's spiritual home is believed to be in the Tatra Mountains, south of Krakow, Poland. This is probably why the eagle has an affinity with Uriel and once when I was journeying, Eagle took me so high that I could see my life below me as a small stream of colour running down the mountainside. As it reached the valley, other souls joined mine and together we wove an amazing tapestry, a rainbow of souls. As we surged down through the valley some were diverted away, but others joined and those who had diverted rejoined us, until we were an enormous rainbow river of light and energy heading towards the sea. "Thus will your life be lived," said Eagle. Eagles eyes are sharp and farseeing just as Uriel sees with his inner sense.

The first angel painting my daughter undertook was that of Uriel. When it was finished, she begged me to take it away. She explained that someone kept prodding her in the side. I told her to ask him to stop! He stopped. Sometimes the answers are so simple, we overlook them!

To work with Uriel, gather three ruby red candles and some crystals such as red jasper, red aqua aura, or rubies if you have them. Burn oils that pertain to Uriel and drink ruby gold charged water containing the Archangel

Uriel essence. It is not easy to find Ruby Gold bottles, and you may have to make your own. I have a superb one that contains real gold; which was made in Malta by Mdina Glass.

Chants to use for Uriel

The river is flowing, flowing and growing,
The river is flowing back to the sea.
Mother Earth carry me
A child I will always be
Mother Earth carry me back to the sea.

The moon she is waning, waxing and waning,
The moon she is waiting for us to be free
Sister Moon shine on me, a child I will always be
Sister Moon shine on me, until I am free.

The energy is flowing, flowing and growing,
The energy is flowing back to the source
Seraphim carry me your servant I will always be
Seraphim carry me back to the source.

Or try this one

Peace is here now,
Within this sphere

Reach out and touch it,
Reach out and feel it
Peace is here – NOW!

Then sit quietly and focus on the painting and play the resonation and allow Uriel to bring peace to your heart, mind and soul.

Uriel says

People of Earth, whenever you light a candle, think of the Earth bathed in peace, knowing peace and experiencing it! When you are troubled, ask me for help and I will come to you and wrap you in my cloak of calm. Together we will encourage peace to spread throughout the world and then throughout the universe. Let the peace within your soul grow until you become peace itself.

Remember to use all your senses other than your eyes. Your ears, your nose, your taste, your feelings and your intuitive self and most of all use your psychic sense, for this is in truth your purest sense. It is for this reason I elected to be blind, so that the psychic senses were truer.

So it is helpful sometimes to shut your eyes and for a while become part of the true world around you. I have sight if I wish it, but by relying on my other senses, I see a truer picture. There is a sight that is beyond sight as you know it, and the more you work with it the more you will know this to be true.

All that work with me help to light the candles of hope in your realm with a brighter light, and as more light them, the greater the power becomes to make changes for the better in your world.

Oils associated with Uriel

HYSSOP *(Hyssopus Officianalis)*
Greater Ray: Ruby Gold
Lesser Ray: Pink
Ruling planet: Jupiter
Element: Fire
Chakras affected: Solar Plexus and the heart
Precautions: You must be careful with this oil. DO NOT
   USE if you are pregnant, epileptic or suffer from
   high blood pressure.
It is believed that Hyssop was offered to Jesus on the cross, by the disciples. It clears the mind and brings a feeling of relaxation and well being. This oil is deemed to be sacred to the Gods and Goddesses. It heightens spirituality and strengthens the mind and is said to cure grief by clearing the spleen. Hyssop brings deep feelings into focus and releases emotional pain.

PATCHOULI *(Pogostomon patchouli)*
Greater Ray: Ruby Gold
Lesser Ray: Golden Yellow
Ruling Planet: Sun or Saturn
Element: Earth
Chakras affected: Base and spleen
Precautions: It can cause loss of appetite and can be
  sedative in low doses, so be careful
This oil grounds and integrates your energies, stops you
from dreaming and helps you ground experiences. Use
it to help you visualize much needed money. It calms
the astral body, clarifies problems and makes the mind
more objective. Makes you aware of reality. Patchouli is
believed to promote peace, fertility and success.

VETIVER *(Vetivaria Zizanoides or Andropogon Muricatus)*
Greater Ray: Ruby gold
Lesser Ray: Golden yellow
Ruling planet: Venus
Element: Earth
Chakras affected: Base and solar plexus
Precautions: None found
Vetiver is a very safe oil and is known as the oil of
tranquillity. It is good for grounding and centring and
brings the chakra system into balance. If the oil is applied
to the solar plexus it prevents one from taking on other

peoples junk, so it is a good protector. Apply physically to the Solar plexus in an anti-clockwise direction or use in the etheric. Vetiver helps balance group meditations and aligns individual energies. It is good for giving you calm, quiet confidence and helps to manifest money in your life.

6

Archangel Chamuel

Chamuel, Chamuel, constant Chamuel,
Bring us into love divine,
Help us turn hatred into love,
And help the world be one with thine.

Chamuel uses the pink ray of divine love. Pink is the higher octave of green and stands for divine unconditional love.

This very important angel often seems to get overlooked, as many of the other angels seem to have more prominence. However if we asked Chamuel about this, he would laugh and say that love is everywhere and tell us that the energy he brings through is what most of us are looking for! Chamuel encourages us to see love everywhere we look, and to spread it wherever we go. In truth, we are love and with it we can overcome all barriers, and we can become the beings of light and love that we are in reality. We can then light the path for others, should they wish to take it.

Chamuel knows no bounds; he works with great subtlety and sometimes with such an immense light that it can knock us off our feet in sheer surprise. He asks us to be merciful to others and to remember that while we are in the human condition, our souls are not so easily perceived (unless we work at it), and so seeing only half of ourselves means we do not appear to be in perfect balance.

Chamuel protects us against harm. What greater protection is there, than love? Love inspires us to our greatest acts of selflessness Love moves us ever forward to greater heights of blissfulness, enabling us to choose better modes of expression. As we give out more love, so we receive more than we have given. Love overcomes all doubts and fears.

Doves represent Chamuel and have been known as a sign of peace and love in many cultures. I always have a dove feather with me whenever I give a reading to remind me to come from the heart. If you can come from the heart in all your dealings you will never go wrong. It is when we fight this and start using logic that we make mistakes and everything goes wrong. Sometimes what we propose to do seems very logical, but if our heart is screaming, "No!" We need to take notice, as our heart is always right. There have been times in my life when everyone else has been telling me not to do a thing, but my heart has been saying that it's right. I have learned the hard way that I need to listen to my heart. When we do this, we find we have more passion for life, and this enables us to get even more out of life. When I started the Cornwall New Age Festival in 1991, my husband thought I had gone totally mad, and he told me every day that I would fall flat on my face. However, being the kind soul he is, he would not let me put up the stalls on my own, so he came and helped me on the day, and then he disappeared! I caught up with him at the end of the day, as the stallholders packed up, and asked him what he thought. "It's great!" he said, "When can we do the next one!" If I had not followed my heart and stuck with it Cornwall New Age Festival would never have been born.

Chamuel means: 'He who sees God', and his spiritual home on Earth is purported to be over St. Louis, Missouri, US.

If you feel up against adversity, ask Chamuel for help and then envisage the heart of the person who appears to be the problem being full of this wonderful pink ray. Let it spread through them and imagine their living space full of love. Do this whenever you have an idle moment as well as making a special time during the day for it. Make sure that you carry it out at least once a day for the next five days and suddenly the situation will magically change.

Once, we had a neighbour, who kept deliberately pushing his cat into our garden to use it as a toilet. Understandably, we complained. He did not take kindly to this and started throwing stones at our house whenever he could. He did no damage, but then one day he tried to run my husband down with his bike. Then to our horror, our beloved postman announced that he was changing his round and that it would be taken over by this neighbour! Imagine our consternation! I started to send the pink ray of love to him. A few days later our old postman returned saying that he had not liked the new round. Our troublesome neighbour moved to another area within a matter of weeks. This is the power of Chamuel.

Chamuel comes to our rescue whenever we ask. I asked for his help one day when my husband knocked a glass coffee machine off a shelf, it hit his arm, cutting through an artery. I realized this when I saw it and drove him to the local hospital. I was so worried that I was driving very badly. When we reached the hospital, I asked for Chamuel's help. As we walked down the long corridor towards the outpatient's section, I noticed something coming towards me. As it came closer, I realized it was a word written in large flaming letters. It said, "LAVENDER." I always carry the oil with me and I realized immediately what Chamuel was saying. I took out the oil and smelt its beautiful aroma, then passing it to my husband to sniff at. We both became calm, as Lavender takes you out of shock. This was just as well, as it was too large a task for our local hospital and I then had to take my husband to our main hospital in Cornwall. However from then on, we were both calm and unworried and were able to continue normally!

To experience Chamuel's energy gather six pink candles, light them and place them with pink crystals such as rose quartz or rhodochrosonite. Burn oils that you have chosen from Chamuel's selection. Sing to build the energy or use singing bowls, or both.

Suggestions to chant are

Chamuel, hear us softly singing
Fill us with your love,
Chamuel let us serve you gladly
Fill us with your love.
Or:
Fill me with your Love by Gila Antara*.

Drink pink charged water containing Chamuel essence. Focus on Chamuel's picture while listening to the Chamuel resonance. Allow your heart to fill with the love and light of the pink ray of divine love. Place your hand on your heart and repeat the following to yourself three times.

I am in my heart,
I am in my heart,
I am in my heart,
I feel with my heart,
I know with my heart,
I am in my heart completely.

Chamuel says

Love is all there is. How many times have you heard this? How many teachers have told you this? Contemplate

---

* *Fill me with your Love* by Gila Antara from "Moondance there is no rush" available from Musik Pool Studio, Isle of Wight

on this and realize that you are love and that you can express this love for the good of the universe. You can overcome all problems, barriers, and adversity using love. Call me if you feel you need help. I, and those who kindly serve me, will hear you and come to your aid. I send to whoever reads these words, love and more love and divine love. We always love you unconditionally. I am with you always.

Oils associated with Chamuel

EUCALYPTUS *(Eucalyptus Globulus)*
Greater Ray: Pink
Lesser Ray: White
Ruling planets: Saturn and Mercury
Element: Air
Chakras affected: Base and heart
Precautions: Epileptics and those with high blood
   pressure are advised to avoid this oil
Eucalyptus protects us from the forces of darkness as it gives off a pale pink emanation that is known as Vyana Vayu. This is believed to light the whole of the human nervous system culminating in the heart. Eucalyptus clears negative energies, especially when people have been arguing or fighting. If massaged into the feet in dilution at night, it gives deep protected sleep. Eucalyptus is

very inspirational and can help you find the answer to a problem by clearing your mind. Always loving and supportive, it blends particularly well with Rose.

PINE *(Pinus Sylvestris)*
Greater Ray: Pink
Lesser Ray: Green
Ruling planets: Saturn or Mars
Element: Air
Chakras affected: Heart and brow
Precautions: Avoid the more toxic species of Pine and note that it may irritate sensitive skin
Pine like Eucalyptus also radiates Vyana Vayu, the liquid light that feeds the nervous system. It clears the mind and refreshes it, especially as Pine makes you breathe more easily. Use it to clear your meditation space, especially after you have been in a crowded place. Pine helps to purify you and strengthen the aura. Calms anxiety. Use it in small doses. It mixes well with Eucalyptus and Lavender.

CYPRESS *(Cupressus sempervirens)*
Greater Ray: Pink
Lesser Ray: Violet
Ruling planet: Saturn
Element: Earth

Chakras affected: Heart and spleen
Precautions: Do not use this oil in pregnancy
It is said that according to an Ancient Babylonian tablet which refers to Cypress oil that it makes evil spirits stand aside and brings through helpful, kindly spirits. Helps with the major changes in life, particularly death. It helps the passage to the afterlife, removes psychic blocks and soothes anger. A comforting oil that brings solace.

YLANG YLANG *(Cananga odorata)*
Greater Ray: Pink
Lesser Ray: Violet
Ruling planet: Venus
Element: Water
Chakras affected: Heart and spleen
Precautions: Be respectful of this oil, as excessive use may lead to nausea and headaches. It could also cause skin irritation and there are those who feel that epileptics should not use it. Overdoing the oil can take you into a different reality, where time moves more slowly
This oil balances the heart beat, the hormones and all the chakras. Creates an aura of peace and protects you. Ylang Ylang eases anger, shock and fear, and gives you space to sort out your problems. It is also very inspirational, I've had some of my best ideas when using Ylang Ylang.

GERANIUM *(Pelargonium Odorantissimum or Graveolens)*
Greater Ray: Pink
Lesser Ray: White
Ruling planet: Venus
Element: Water
Chakras affected: Heart and base
Precautions: Avoid this oil if you are pregnant and be careful if you use the pill or HRT. It can cause irritation to sensitive skin

Geranium balances the emotions and the hormones and is good to use at night as it helps you to sleep. This oil is uplifting and balances the mind, reducing stress, promoting happiness and giving protection. Protect your home by you using it on a burner. Blends well with Lavender.

7

Archangel Michael

Magnificent Michael with your sword of light
When all seems lost we call to you,
Help us turn our wrongs to rights
Protect us with your ray of blue.

The Archangel Michael uses the blue ray of power, protection and truth. This ray is the energy that defends the right, the innocent and the confused. This ray maintains balance and can interfere when the balance of power is lost. It brings freedom from doubt and fear and is inspiring. He is regarded as the prince of angels and his name means 'One who is like God'. Azure or electric blue is the higher octave of blue and stands for divine will, let go and let God.

Michael works with us constantly, divesting us of things we no longer need that block our sight, hearing and capability of understanding. As we grow spiritually, we can allow Michael to take away the things that no longer serve us. Michael is the angel who cuts away the things that we no longer need. He can see the bigger picture and often takes away things that we cling to because we mistakenly believe that we still need them. He has great compassion, which he shows to us at all times. He is like the loving parent whose child is suffering from toothache. The child does not want to go to the dentist, but the loving parent takes him anyway, knowing that as soon as the tooth is dealt with, the child will feel better. The child however can only see the pain and so objects mightily, until it is all over, when all is well again. This is the way that Michael treats us, he knows the things in our lives that we no longer need and does his best to remove them from us. He knows they are detrimental to us. We however do not, and like the crying child we cling desperately to them, unaware of the greater picture. Thus it is that when we go through a 'Michael' time, it can be full of frustrations and seeming setbacks. It is only later when we look back that we realize that we needed to lose these things, but at the time we could not comprehend the reasons why. It is we who put the blocks in the way and tend to make the experience painful. Michael gently but firmly removes the blocks bit by bit. It is we who agonize over losing someone or something. Michael will then remind us that nothing in the world is ever lost, it is impossible to lose anything.

We constantly hold ourselves back by hanging on to people, objects, situations etc. Sometimes we do not possess the wisdom to see that some are detrimental to us. Michael CAN see the true picture and so to aid us he uses the sword of truth to cut away what we no longer need.

Michael's eyes are full of compassion and understanding; he is an angel to call on in times of great pressure. I had occasion to do this once, when I was asked to speak at an Angel Conference. Michael had told me that he wanted me to speak about him but what was more he wanted me to chant to build the energy, as the Michael

line* ran very close to the place the conference was be-
ing held. The Michael line is a line of energy that runs
through Britain. Often churches found on the line are
dedicated to St Michael. When I arrived I realized it
was a theatre with spotlights and microphones, to which
I was unaccustomed. In fact the very thought made my
knees shake and butterflies of enormous size seemed to
take over my stomach! I headed for the Ladies, and once
there, I begged Michael for help, as I felt unable to do
what he asked of me. I then walked round the numerous
stalls for a while, when suddenly a great calm descended
upon me and I knew that I could do what was needed.

Michael strengthens us and enables us to take up our
power; he frees us from doubt and fear and gives us faith
in ourselves. Many people have asked for his protection
and liken it to the feeling of being wrapped in a soft
blue cloak, that keeps you safe and secure. It is a cloak
of peace of mind.

Michael carries the sword of truth, and many light
workers discover that they are carrying this sword. At
one time I worked with a group of people in Cornwall
who met on a regular basis to meditate together. One
night we all received messages concerning a sword. I
received a poem about a sword, which I only managed

---

* See *The Sun and the Serpent* by Paul Broadhurst and Hamish Miller,
Pendragon Press.

to write down scraps of, but others received impressions of places that it was felt we needed to visit. So in the following weeks we would go and visit the various sacred places that came up in our meditations. The last one we needed to go to was Carn Brae and we went there on Midsummer's Eve. We did a meditation for peace in Bosnia and we linked in with friends from Germany at the same time. During the meditation, I and some of the others saw a large sword coming towards us, which disappeared over us. We speculated on what it could mean, and ended up looking at a map of Cornwall, which was marked with all the sites we had visited. Someone decided to join them all up, whereupon, it was discovered that this also formed a sword.

I thought no more about it until, I got up next morning and went to do my morning exercises and found that I could hardly move my right shoulder. When I put my hand up to it I could feel a sword on my shoulder in a scabbard. As you can imagine, I was not best pleased and I found during the following days that it would cause painful twinges when I was carrying out massages. I kept telling myself that I was imagining it, and eventually decided to go for some kinesiology to see if I could clear it.

Imagine my amazement when the kinesiologist asked me if I knew that I was carrying a large sword! She tried to remove it, and was partly successful in that she took it away for the time I was in her room, but I knew she would be unable to do so for good and I was right. As I left the room I felt it come back into position on my shoulder. Years later, I met up with the amazing spiritual teacher Sandy Stevenson*, who explained the connection of the sword to Michael. She told me that one day I would need to use the sword and that when I did, I would find that Michael would send power through his sword into mine.

One day a young man came to me asking for healing, and as soon as I put my hands on him, I knew that the he had special healing powers that needed awakening. I knew instinctively that it was time to draw the sword. I did, and when Michael's sword touched mine, an energy that seemed like lightning coursed through me into the young man. He told me later that it was like being 'lit up' or connected to an electricity supply. He later became a very strong healer and channeller.

There are many stories told about Michael, how he has defended the weak and those who have prayed to him for help. In a well-documented story about the First World War, Michael appeared with his legions and drove the Germans back. The British could not understand

---

* Sandy Stevenson is a spiritual teacher and author of *The Awakener*, ISBN 1-85860-040-5 Gateway/McMillan Ireland.

why they ran, and eventually caught up with one of the German soldiers, who said that an army in white had come charging at them on horseback. When fired upon, nothing happened, they just came charging on. At the front was a man in white with a halo. The Germans turned and ran. During this time the British had seen nothing except the Germans running for some unknown reason. This story is apparently documented in British and German annals and is known as the miracle of the white cavalry at Ypres. This is an example of the way Michael can interfere once the balance of power is lost.

Michael is also of help when you start to doubt yourself, or feel you have lost your way. Sometimes to make sure I'm on the right track, I ask for a sign to prove it to myself. One day I asked Michael to show me a UFO to let me know I was going along the right path. A few nights later, I woke in the middle of the night. I lay there wondering what had woken me, when I saw this bright light moving through the Venetian blinds. I realized that it was too bright for a planet and grew curious, so I leapt across the bed, and put my fingers between the slats and peered out. To my amazement, this huge bright light suddenly broke apart and formed the shape of a four leaf clover! I looked away for a second to open the blinds so I could see better, and when I looked back it was gone! It was then that I realized Michael had sent the sign I asked for. Whenever you doubt yourself, do not be afraid to ask for a sign and let it be something that you choose for yourself.

His spiritual home is believed to be near Banff and Lake Louise in Canada. Electric Blue or Azure is the higher octave and stands for divine will.

To experience Michael's energy, use chants such as

> We are the power in everyone,
> We are the dance of the moon and the sun
> We are the hope that will never hide
> We are the turning of the tide.

Or use the following song, which is sung to the tune of *Michael Row the Boat Ashore:*

> Michael come to us this day, Alleluia!
> Michael light us on our way, Alleluia,
>
> Michael with your sword of light, Alleluia!
> Help us see with second sight, Alleluia.
>
> Michael, cut away our strife, Alleluia,
> Help us lead a better life, Alleluia.
>
> Michael hear us when we pray, Alleluia!
> For strength and courage through the day, Alleluia.
>
> Michael with your cloak of blue, Alleluia!
> Protect us please, the whole day through, Alleluia.

Drink blue charged water laced with Michael essence and light one blue candle. Use blue crystals such as lapis lazuli sodalite or azurite. Place Michael's oils on your oil burner. Consider something, someone or a situation in your life that you would like to be free of, and write it down on a piece of paper. Keep it in your hand as you play the resonation of Michael, and keep your focus on the painting. Quieten your mind and allow yourself to experience his energy. Ask for his help with your problem. Ask for protection if you feel in need of it. Afterwards, cut the piece of paper into small pieces and throw them away.

Michael says

Be true to yourself and work on discovering who you really are. Realize your power and accept who you are. Have compassion for others; remember that you, too, were once in their position. You are the creator of your universe. Have courage and use it to change things for the better, help others to realize their power and strength. Call me if you would see and know the truth and it will be revealed to you.

Oils associated with Michael are

FRANKINCENSE *(Boswellia Carteri/Thurifera)*
Greater Ray: Blue
Lesser Ray: Golden yellow
Ruling planet: Sun
Element: Air
Chakras affected: Throat and crown
Precautions: It is a very safe oil, but of course should still be used with respect.

Frankincense gives power and wisdom. Believed to be associated with the God Aeolus (The God of the winds) and the breath of life. Frankincense lifts the veil of Maya or illusion that is reputed to descend upon us at the moment of birth. This is why it was believed to have been taken to Jesus at His birth. I have certainly used the oil at the births of my grandchildren and can only say that it is true, the child takes life without any force in any way. The first time I used it the midwife was amazed at its action, and I ended up giving her my bottle of Frankincense. It is a calming oil that promotes deep tranquility and is also used for rejuvenation. This is possibly because it makes you feel so serene that the years drop off you! Frankincense helps you cut the ties with the past, which is why it is so linked to Michael. Patricia Davis states that you can use it in the bath to wash away old patterns. It is helpful during times of change, and is aromatherapy's answer to the Walnut flower essence.

Take it to the birth of a child, as I did with my grandsons, and put it under their noses as soon as the child is born and they take life immediately with no concern and maybe they will be able to remember why they came here.

SANDALWOOD *(Santalum Album)*
Greater Ray: Blue
Lesser Ray: Golden yellow
Ruling planet: Saturn although some say the Moon
Element: Water
Chakras affected: Base and crown
Precautions: Sandalwood is reputed to be the mildest of oils, although I have come across the odd person who is allergic to it, so perhaps wisest to muscle test first. Neither is it the oil to use when depressed as it can take you even lower

Sandalwood is very useful for meditation, stilling the mental chatter and allowing the mind to move into deeper states, whilst keeping you grounded. This oil is also helpful in cutting ties with the past and helps you to open to a greater spirituality. You can protect yourself by using this oil on the third eye and the vertebra that stands out on your neck when you bend your head over. It is of course better known for its use in perfume.

CHAMOMILE *(Matricaria Chamomilla)*
Greater Ray: Blue
Lesser Ray: Golden yellow
Ruling planet: Venus, although others say the Moon
Element: Water
Chakra affected: Throat
Precautions: Chamomile should be avoided in the early
   months of pregnancy
The Ancient Egyptians dedicated Chamomile to the sun, it was much used in Egypt and used as part of their embalming processes. The oil was thought to unite body and soul, and this is apparent when you use it, as it brings deep calm to the mind, thus enabling you to connect again to your higher self. Very good aid for meditation; helps you to reach the right state of mind to bring about a deeper relaxation, thus enabling you to find a greater understanding. Chamomile was reputed to be one of the healing herbs that Odin (the Norse God) gave to the people.

8

Archangel Raphael

Raphael, Raphael radiant Raphael,
Help us heal ourselves and others,
Show to us the truth unbidden,
Help us to see all that is hidden.

Raphael is associated with the Green ray of Healing and Truth. The Green ray is a ray of love and understanding, and those who work with this energy are healers. Many acknowledge that they are healers but there are others who go about the healing process innocently and are happy just to feel that they have lifted someone's spirits. They often go through life unaware of how much healing they bring. Such a man was my father, who always had time to listen, and this in itself is very healing. His credo was 'So live that when you die, even the undertaker will be sorry!' At his funeral I was amazed, so many people came from all over Cornwall, mostly to shake my hand and tell me what a wonderful man he was. He worked on the Green ray and I'm sure Raphael touched him some time in his life. He was so loving and kind.

Raphael was the first Archangel I experienced. I say experienced because Raphael does not like to be seen. He is often glimpsed by nurses in hospitals but never seen fully. I experienced him one day when I was giving healing to an old Cornish gentleman who had had a stroke; he had lost the use of his left arm and had problems with his left leg as well. I started working on him as usual, (I had been going to see him for some time) when the both of us were surrounded in a golden light and I knew without a doubt that I stood within the angel Raphael. To make sure I mentally asked if this was Raphael and was told that it was so. It was like standing in pure bliss, in fact it is very hard to find words to describe it. Occasionally odd thoughts would come to me, 'Does the old man see him as well?' 'How long should I stay here?' I realized much later, that it was my ego that was coming in and trying to distract me from this wonderful experience! However on this day my ego was going nowhere. I was enjoying the experience so much I wanted to stay there forever or until Raphael chose to leave, which of course he eventually did. As soon as he had gone, the old man turned to me and said "That were an angel, weren't it?" I told him that it was, and that he must be going to get better, and so he did. Within a month, he had regained the use of his arm and leg. Later I also remembered that this particular gentleman had been very kind to me about 10 years previously, and had helped me out on several occasions. The last time I had seen him, as I walked away, I wished that I could do something to repay his kindness. I was so poor at the time that I could not even afford to buy him a box of chocolates. I had looked back at him, and thought to myself that perhaps one day I would find some way of repaying him. It seems to me now that I did. Perhaps we need to remember that saying about being careful what you wish for, as you may get it! I'm glad that I did get the chance to repay him.

After I had seen the angel, I walked away from the old man's house on air. I felt very excited and amazed that this had happened to me. I suddenly felt that I wanted to tell someone, but it suddenly hit me that if I did they would probably think me totally mad. Everyone I met in the next few days I looked at with interest and weighed up whether or not they could cope with hearing about the experience. In every case I felt I could not tell them. I did manage to tell my younger daughter, but it was to be many years before I could bring myself to tell other people about it.

Raphael works very close to the earth, and brings healing to anyone who will acknowledge him. He works on healing the planet and we need to remember that 'as above so below', and until we set ourselves to rights, we cannot set the world to rights. His healing energy helps the body, mind, soul and spirit. It is said he also tries to repair the rifts between nations. His retreat is reputedly Fatima, Portugal. I also wonder about Crete, but this is said to be the retreat of The Master Hilarion who also works on the Green Ray.

When my daughter worked on this painting, she found it very difficult, and she phoned me and told me that she could not paint him from the front, no matter what she did! I agreed and told her that he hated to be seen, so this is why he is shown side on. Many people tell me that he is carrying the cross of Christ, and in some lights this does seem to be the case.

When Neil H first recorded his CD *Resonation of Angels*, he set up the recording and played all the way through. When he played it back the resonation of Raphael was not there! Neil knew that the equipment was working and if it had been turned off it would not have recorded Jophiel, but Jophiel was there. So we had a special workshop to record the resonations with both of us present.

His name means 'God cures' or 'God has healed', and in the Apocrypha it is Raphael who cures Tobias' blindness. Raphael is the angel of healing and truth, and it is often when we realize the truth that we become healed. So sometimes it is needful that we do our best to find the truth within us, for when we can face this with love in our hearts, our pain dissolves.

It's when we come to terms with the real truth that we are healed. Raphael helps us with this process. His energy is gentle and loving, but also strong and unquenchable. Many people on the planet work with this energy, bringing solace to those who suffer. They often work in the hidden manner of Raphael, quietly bringing healing to everyone they touch or have dealings with. He has legions of angels on Earth as well as in spirit, peacefully forging ahead bringing about change imperceptibly.

It is often a while after Raphael has passed by and changed the situation that you realize he was there and just catch a glimpse of his back receding in the distance. His touch is subtle but life changing, and once he has placed his gentle hand upon you, believe me, life is never ever the same again! It is hard to describe this gentle, tranquil, subtle, whispering energy that treats you as if you are the finest porcelain. When Raphael touches you, you know you are treasured and appreciated. He is often the quiet stranger who appears to come from nowhere, who helps you out of a situation. When you try to picture his face afterwards, you cannot focus on it at all.

To work with the energy of Raphael, find a quiet space, if possible outside, under trees. Use crystals such as malachite and green calcite. Light five green candles, and use singing bowls or drums to connect more deeply. Drink green charged water containing Raphael essence and burn oils associated with the angel.

Chants to sing for Raphael

Trees

Trees are good for the soul,
Trees are good for the soul,
Trees are good for the soul,
Bless them with your love.

Trees are our guardians,
Trees are our guardians,
Trees are our guardians
Bless them with your love

I bless all the trees,
I bless all the trees,
I bless all the trees,
I bless them with my love

Or try this one to the tune of *Fly like an Eagle.*

Fly Like An Angel

Fly like an angel, fly so high,
Circling the universe on wings of pure light,
Hey! Healing angel, shine your light on me
Hey healing angel, shine your light on me.

Concentrate on his picture as you listen to the resonation. Let yourself sink deeply into meditation and ask Raphael to help you heal yourself.

Raphael says

I am always ready to help those who truly seek healing. I am patient and will wait until you are ready. However, once you have asked for help, I can intervene more powerfully. I always do my best to bring about healing in as gentle a way as possible. This is not always possible; sometimes it needs to be quick, and this can shock you and cause pain. However beloved, I would never cause you pain unnecessarily. Once you have been healed, I would wish you to turn your eyes and hearts to the planet and join with me in bringing about healing all over Earth. Together we can move mountains, we can bring about a peace the like of which has never yet been seen on Earth. Go with my blessing.

Oils associated with Raphael

BERGAMOT *(Citrus Bergamia)*
Greater Ray: Green
Lesser Ray: Yellow
Ruling planet: Sun although some say Mercury
Element: Air
Chakras affected: Crown, brow and heart
Precautions: You need to be careful of this oil if you are
   going out in the sun, as it is phototoxic.

This oil allays anger and frustration and is uplifting. It helps you to radiate joy and is calming and balancing and relieves tension. Bergamot will clear the aura of negativity and protect the aura from harmful influences. It creates confidence and boosts motivation and can be used to increase the flow of money into your life. Also helpful for those who refuse to look at their problems and hide them away in odd corners of the body. It gives them strength to look at the problem and deal with it. Bergamot is an oil that lights up your life and brings a greater depth and understanding.

PEPPERMINT *(Mentha Piperita)*
Greater Ray: Green
Lesser Ray: Blue
Ruling planet: Mercury although some say Venus
Element: Air
Chakras affected: Throat and brow
Precautions: Be careful not to use this oil if you are
   taking homeopathic remedies, or even put it close to
   the remedies, as it is an antidote to them. Peppermint
   discourages the flow of milk in nursing mothers.
   Avoid it during pregnancy as well.
Peppermint helps to clear rubbish from the mind, making you think more clearly and concentrate. It relieves states of anger and helps to dispel pride and

overcome feelings of inferiority. Stops negative thoughts and is useful for self-purification. A very motivational oil. It makes you more perceptive and helps you live for the moment, bringing a clarity and glow with it. Peppermint is also very inspirational.

ROSE *(Rosa Centifolia)*
Greater Ray: Green
Lesser Ray: Pink
Ruling planet: Venus
Element: Water
Chakras affected: Brow and heart
Precautions: Avoid the oil in pregnancy
This oil is believed to create a greater connection with the angelic realms than other oils. It helps to make women more positive, and helps heal and open the heart chakra. The Rose is believed to be the favourite of the angels, and was a symbol of the Virgin Mary, but this was taken away because of its connection with Aphrodite. It creates confidence and rids us of self-doubt. It also promotes passion and fulfilment.

9

Archangel Jophiel

Jophiel, Jophiel, joyful Jophiel,
To you we pray when sense is clouded,
To you we pray when dreams are shrouded,
Please clear our thoughts and clear our vision,
So we may think with sharp precision.

The Archangel Jophiel is the angel of wisdom; he uses the golden yellow ray to send his vibrations to us and to allow us to tap into the universal wisdom. I always feel that he is a joyful spirit and I often call him joyful Jophiel! His name actually means 'Beauty of God'. He tells me that wisdom gained through laughter is more easily remembered and has more substance to it. So, he prefers us to learn in a way that is full of fun and one that draws us into the subject. If you think about it, it is often easier to recall events that were hilarious, and we remember small details because the event was so full of laughter. He is therefore asking us to make our lives more meaningful by being joyful and living our lives to the full, so that we become more positive and consequently we attract even more positive experiences. He brings us the information in a method that suits us best, so if we respond to sound, then he will use sound, or whatever sense is appropriate for us. He also points out that we do not need to remember everything, we just have to tune in to the universal wisdom, whereupon the answer will come to us. Of course this takes time and patience, but if we practice we can learn to tune in easily and quickly. Asking for Jophiel's help allows us access even faster. Jophiel is the angel to call on when we are doing exams or tests of any kind, or simply in a situation where we do not know what to do for the best.

I found myself in this position when I was seeking a

way of bringing the angelic energies through to us in an easier manner, one in which very little explanation was needed. I therefore decided to journey to Jophiel's realm and ask him for advice. He assured me that there was a way and suggested making angelic essences. When I said I had no idea how to make them, he referred me to the Archangel Zadkiel. (See chapter on Zadkiel).

I keep a small picture of Jophiel on the wall in my workroom, and I turn to it whenever my memory fails me! He is not so well known as some of the archangels, but this does not mean he is any less powerful.

The golden yellow ray of divine wisdom vibrates to the higher octave of violet and is the colour that allows us access to the greater cosmic wisdom. When we vibrate to this ray we have a greater understanding of the bigger picture. We become aware that there is an understanding that is greater than our own and that sometimes we have to trust to God and the angels, because they can see the larger vista. Things that happen to us sometimes make us wonder what is going on, but if we trust and allow things to unfold naturally we find that often we will have gained something much greater.

Jophiel is also the angel of illumination, and this power allows us to see ourselves and others as we truly are. He also illuminates the path for us and is our guiding light when we walk through that 'valley of the shadow of death', or whenever we reach a bad patch in our lives. Jophiel directs us and cheers us on. He inspires us. He has a wonderful sense of humor which he uses to help us make light of problems. As soon as we lighten up our problems become less and we can view them from a different perspective. When things are brought out into the light, they no longer have the same power over us and are immediately less frightening.

You have probably noticed that when artists draw the saints or Jesus, they place a golden halo around them. This is because the artists are honoring their great wisdom and their work on the golden ray. People with a great deal of wisdom always have a golden aura, which most psychics can see. Many years ago, I remember seeing such an aura at a workshop at the Mind, Body and Spirit Festival in London. The lady concerned obviously had great wisdom. Unfortunately I had never seen an aura so clearly before, and I became so entranced by it as it flowed and reformed around her as she moved across the stage that I never heard a word of the lecture!

I used to visit one of my first spiritual teachers at classes in her own house. One day, discussing an exercise with another of the students, I realized that the walls in the room where our class was held were white. I had always seen them as yellow. I then realized that I was seeing her aura!

Jophiel's spiritual retreat on Earth is reputed to be near Lanchow north central China.

To tune in to Jophiel and experience the golden ray of wisdom, find a quiet space, where you will not be disturbed, and light two golden yellow candles, place oils associated with Jophiel on an oil burner and drink golden yellow charged water. Use yellow crystals such as citrine and iron pyrites.

Use chants such as

Joyful Jophiel
Jophiel, Jophiel, joyful Jophiel,
Jophiel, Jophiel, angel of joy
Fill us with your wisdom Jophiel
Fill us with your bounteous joy.

Or try
Trust your own thinking by Gila Antara from 'Moondance there is no rush'

Or try this African chant,
Noyana
Noyana, Noyana,
Noyana, Noyana,
Nithini Noyana,
Noyana peh Zulu.

Listen to the Jophiel resonance and focus on Jophiel's picture and allow yourself to get in touch with his wisdom.

Jophiel says

Let me light your path, let me help you find the best way forward for you. Tune in and meditate with me daily, so that I may show you the path to wisdom and help you deal with the problems that prevent you from experiencing the light. Call upon me and I will light your path through the storm if you trust in me.

The oils associated with the golden yellow ray are

CLARY SAGE *(Salvia Sclarea)*
Greater Ray: Golden yellow
Lesser Ray: Blue
Ruling planet: Mercury
Element: Air
Chakras affected: Crown and throat
Precautions: This oil is very potent and can send you to
   sleep so do not drink alcohol or drive when using it.
Clary Sage puts you in touch with the dream world and enhances dream recall. Used before sleep, it can help focus on a problem and give you the answer through a dream. It helps to strengthen the inner eye and helps us to 'see' more clearly. It brings tranquility of mind and allows you space to consider. A balancing rejuvenating oil.

MARJORAM *(Origanum marjoram)*
Greater Ray: Golden yellow
Lesser Ray: Violet
Ruling planet: Mercury
Element: Air
Chakras affected: Crown and spleen
Precautions: Avoid using during pregnancy. Can cause
   drowsiness

Marjoram soothes anxiety, especially that linked with grief. It is known as the oil of celibacy and helps those who are celibate, however it is not recommended that you use it for long periods of time as it inhibits normal response. The oil warms the emotions and calms the astral body and promotes peace. It helps the unification of the psychic and conscious minds. Take care not to inhale marjoram too strongly as it can put you to sleep.

MYRRH *(Commiphora Myrrha)*
Greater Ray: Golden yellow
Lesser Ray: White
Ruling planet: Sun whilst others feel it is Saturn
Element: Water
Chakras affected: Crown and base
Precautions: Avoid it in pregnancy

It has the ability to preserve tissue, which is why it was used in embalming, so it helps to keep you young. Myrrh was used by the ancient Egyptians at Heliopolis in the Sun Rituals held at noon every day. The oil strengthens the psychic centers, mind and spirituality and helps clear apathy and awaken spiritual awareness about the spiritual reasons behind everyday existence. It is believed that no soldier of ancient Greece went to war without carrying Myrrh. The reason for this was that it not only helped heal wounds, but also gave courage to do what had to be done.

BASIL *(Ocimum Basilicum)*
Greater Ray: Golden yellow
Lesser Ray: Violet
Ruling planet: Mars
Element: Fire
Chakras affected: Crown and spleen
Precautions: Avoid the oil in pregnancy. Some may find it a skin irritant and used to excess it is stupefying

The scent of Basil lifts the spirits and refreshes the mind. It helps you to focus and stay focused. Good to use when you are feeling down. This oil helps you to make good decisions and helps you choose the correct path. Sharpens the senses so good to use before meditation. It creates balance.

10

The Angel Princes

The Angel Princes, as I explained in the chapter on the hierarchy, are the angels that look after towns, countries and nations. They are the angels that can cause change for the better, if we remember to ask them. These are the angels that help the people of an area have an identity, they are like the parents of a huge family. They encourage us to live in peace and harmony with our neighbors and do their best to create a place that best suits the needs of the inhabitants.

Unfortunately we human beings can be very unappreciative. If we have no love for the Earth and the countryside, we end up building cement jungles and this cuts us off from the energies that we need. We need to feel the earth beneath our feet, as we draw energy from it that helps keep us balanced and healthy. Once we stop touching the earth because it is underneath a layer of cement we cease to be able to draw that energy into our system and so our system slowly becomes unbalanced and we become ill.

I remember some years ago a man who worked in the farming industry coming to me for a treatment. He said that his back was aching as he had just returned from an exhibition in Birmingham where all the floors were made of cement. He told me that after several days of standing on it talking to potential customers, his back had really begun to hurt. He also added that even the cattle did not like it and reacted by being miserable and irritable, even though straw had been put down for them.

Next time you have to stand on cement for quite some time, take the time to notice how you feel and see if your back starts to ache. It may take some time but eventually you will notice a difference.

Of course when we become separated from the earth's energy source, we also begin to lose our connection with spirit. This makes our feeling of disconnection even worse and tends to be the time when we lose our sense of self. We become fearful because we no longer feel secure.

This of course causes a huge problem for the Angel Princes, because once we lose our security and become fearful, we also begin to be suspicious of others' actions, and so a spiral begins that takes us further away from our objectives.

Obviously the answer is to do our best to make contact with the earth as much as possible, by walking out each day on the land at sometime. This is easy for those of us who live in the country, but for those in the cities it means visiting parks and gardens if we are to maintain our contact. The only other alternative is to make sure we 'ground' ourselves daily.

Grounding is an exercise where we imagine energy coming up from the earth and filling our root chakra with energy. Chakras are the energy centres throughout our body that draw in energy for our use; they are like spinning wheels of colour. It is when these centres get blocked that the body becomes imbalanced, and if this continues then illness can result. There are many chakras throughout the body, but there are seven main chakras and they use the seven colours of the rainbow. Thus:

Root Chakra – Red
Sacral Chakra – Orange
Solar Plexus Chakra – Yellow
Heart Chakra – Green
Throat Chakra – Blue
Brow Chakra – Indigo
Crown Chakra – Violet

These of course then correspond to the archangels as each one is connected to the higher octave of the colours, e.g. Gabriel works on the white ray, which is the higher octave of red.

Normally we take energy from the earth, which fills our root chakra with energy, this then spirals up to the sacral chakra, the solar plexus chakra and into the heart. We also take energy from spirit (or God, or in Native American parlance, Father Sky). This energy spirals down through the crown chakra and into the brow and throat chakras where it continues on down to the heart chakra. Here it meets the energy from the earth and the two combine and keep us emotionally balanced. When we are not receiving these energies as we should, we become 'ungrounded'.

This of course is very unhelpful for the Angel Princes, for it means we have lost contact with them as well. It also means that we lose respect for ourselves and when this happens we cease to have respect for others and for our surroundings. We can see this happening around us. Years ago when people were more connected to the Earth, we looked after her with more care and respect.

For a moment consider Switzerland. The Swiss look after their country with far more care than most of us. I remember seeing a tourist drop some litter on the quay as we waited for a ferry on Lake Lucerne. The lady from the kiosk came bustling out and picked it up immediately, making sure that the culprit knew that he had offended. The Swiss are a nation who are respected by others.

We can ground ourselves in many ways, we can learn disciplines such as T'ai Chi or Arab Egyptian dance. We can hug trees. Most of all we need to start respecting the Earth. We can do this by starting to take a pride in ourselves and our appearance and everything that we do. If we put love into every action we take, it is brought back to us at least threefold and we gain respect for ourselves. We then feel more confident and are able to give even more respect, love and understanding.

This is what our Angel Princes aspire to create in us. When we go out into the countryside or to the seaside, it often fills us with awe as we take in the incredible beauty of the Earth. This makes us stop and think, it gives us time to stop and stare. When we do this we are connecting with spirit and allowing that energy to fill us, whilst at the same time we are receiving the Earth energies and so it creates a greater balance within us.

The Angel Princes hold dominion over all of the nature spirits, elementals and devas. They all work together to bring about the best outcome for the Earth. This of course does not always go down well with the humans, who often work against this and towards lining their own pockets to the detriment of every other living being. The Princes also work with every colour imaginable, using them to help create a better place for us. We humans tend to choose colours that we feel represent our nation or country, such as the red, white and blue of the Union Jack flag of Great Britain and the Angel Princes then use these colours to help us. Red is a very grounding colour and white is a very spiritual one. Blue helps us to communicate and create understanding and truth. So all three together say that we as a people are doing our best to bring about a better spiritual understanding on Earth.

The Angel Princes must at times have despaired of us, or come very close to it, although the angels never give up on us. It is time that we took up our rightful task on Earth of working for and with her, protecting her and increasing her beauty. In some parts of the Earth we are like spoilt children demanding more and more and giving nothing in return. Of course we are not all like this, but the more of us that start to work with the Angel Princes, the more we can bring about a change in the attitude of those who have lost their connection with Earth.

How do we do this? We have many choices. We can start by just hugging a tree and doing our best to communicate with it, or by growing flowers or vegetables.

We can go out into the countryside and sing, chant and dance. It is good to go to the once sacred places like Stonehenge. In Cornwall, we have three stone circles on Bodmin Moor that are known as the Hurlers. This is a very sacred place and has its own guardian. If you go to one of these places to revere the land, remember to ask permission of the guardian of the circle before entering.

I remember once visiting this circle with my husband and dog. My husband merrily marched into the circle with the dog, but I stopped and asked permission mentally. Immediately a small breeze surrounded me and gently blew the hood on my coat so that it covered my head. I then entered the circle and started to travel around it from stone to stone in the way I was directed to move. It is important in these places to stop and listen and feel with your heart. I was about three stones along when a massive hailstorm hit us. My husband took the full force, he tried to put up his umbrella but it blew inside out immediately. I continued to move around the circle as directed, but the side I was on afforded me protection from the stones. I saw that my husband was having problems so I moved more quickly to try and help him, but as soon as I reached him the storm stopped and the sun came out!

I hope this demonstrates to you that it is in your best interests to ask for permission to enter and to follow your heart about which path to take once you have gained entry!

To work with the Angel Princes there are many ways that are available to you. You can meditate and talk with them, but there are other ways that they prefer.

Some years ago I worked with a group of people who were working together to help Earth in many ways. Cornwall at that time was one of the poorest parts of the UK and I believe it still is although many things have changed. We were told that we needed to do a certain dance to awaken the dragon energy that was hidden in Cornwall. This we were told would bring back Cornwall's riches and lift off a pattern that was holding Cornwall back from being all that she could be. We were given instructions for the dance and told to perform it on a certain hill where many of Cornwall's kings were crowned.

We all agreed to do this and on a cold miserable December day, we set off for the designated place. Imagine our horror when it turned out to be a place that was in full view of a busy road with traffic rushing past! However, we had agreed to do what was asked of us and so we formed a circle to do so. My husband is not a dancer and refused to take part, but he thrust his staff, which contained a large crystal at the top, into the ground in the centre, he then retired to the field with his camera to take pictures of us as we danced. We started to dance and as it was a cold day it was good to build the energy and get warm. Eventually our dance came to a close and as we all stood there breathless from our exertions, the sun appeared for one moment and lit the crystal in my husband's staff. He saw this happen and took a picture of it! He said that it was truly amazing and that the photograph did not do it justice because it was an incredible blaze of light that the camera was unable to capture.

We felt that we had achieved what was asked and we noticed that from this point Cornwall's economy began to improve. The Eden Project began shortly after and that has brought a great deal of wealth to our small land. We have also received what is called 'Objective One' funding which gives businesses money to help them expand.

The Angel Princes like us to dance and also to sing. They particularly like us to chant and it is good if you can persuade others to go with you into the countryside to do so. It is best if you can find a sheltered place where you can light a candle and surround it with crystals of all kinds, because they are from the Earth. Amber is also very acceptable, amber being the petrified resin from pine trees. Amber helps to balance all the chakras. You may use oils if you wish and the ones that I would suggest are Amber, Petitgrain, Juniper and Black Spruce. However, most oils are acceptable as they come from plants or trees, which are part of the Angel Princes' domain. It is up to you to use you intuition.

The dance that we were given is to form a circle and join hands but keep your elbows bent, then step sideways for 15 paces moving you arms backwards and forwards. After the fifteenth pace, step forward, swing your arms up and shout Hai Ra! Then move to the right sideways for nine paces, moving your arms as before and after the ninth pace step back swinging your arms back and down and shout Mei Ra! Repeat this 15 times.

The Angel Princes tell us that this dance helps to release various patterns that are no longer any use to the people who reside on this planet.

If you choose to sing or chant you may use anything you feel appropriate to the Angel Princes. My suggestions would be the chant 'Trees' (see Raphael's chapter) or 'Peace is here' (see Uriel's chapter) or you could amend the first verse of Angels Hear us and sing it this way:

Angels hear us softly calling
Fill us with your love
Angels help us serve you gladly
Help us heal the Earth.

You will know instinctively when to stop chanting this and just allow yourself to be part of the place you have chosen, feel its energy and ask if there is anything you can do to help this particular place or any way in which you can serve the Angel Princes.

You may not get any answers then, but ideas may come to you later and also sometimes come in dreams.

The Princes also gave me a song, which sometimes I just speak aloud, as it is a positive affirmation that reminds us of our place in the universe. This is how it was given to me and I would like to point out that Kernow is the old name for Cornwall and you could change this to the name of the area that you live in.

I am safe and well
And Kernow thrives and prospers
Wherever I am beauty surrounds me
The angelic energy supports and protects me
And everything I touch is enhanced by angelic
    energy that flows through me
Earth grows and glows in beauty
Our Solar system moves in strength and beauty
The universe resounds in beauty.
I am part of the sound
I am the sound
I am the sound.

The Angel Princes have also given me guidelines for living and I will repeat these here for you now:

1. Do your best to ease pain and suffering wherever it is found. Accept that some will be unable to receive help, but you can still place them in a positive sphere of love and light. (Their suggestion is a pink sphere turning one way with a white sphere turning the other, but you may use whatever you feel is best).

2. Pay attention to the care and welfare of the body that houses you. There are many pressures to come and to withstand them you need to care for your body with love and affection. Feed it foods that are enjoyable and enable your body to function properly and stay away from substances that cause its erosion. Use oils to protect and nurture it. Clothe it in bright colours and beautiful materials, make your body feel loved and cared for. Above all respect and be grateful to your body because it allows you to see, hear, feel and touch everything around you. It allows you movement and if you look after it well, it will serve you for many, many years.

3. Meditation is important and efforts need to be made to include it every day in your daily affairs, to enable us (spirit) to form stronger bonds with you.

4. Create a positive space and aura around you, and keep it that way. Understand the power of speech and

that the words you say become reality. Make the space you reside in as positive as possible, clearing out anything that does not resonate positively with you.

5. Fun. Bring as much laughter into your life as possible. Do your best to make everything in your life exciting and fun. Do everything with a passion for life. Think up ways of bringing people together where they may laugh together and have fun. Sing together, dance together, play team games together, there are many alternatives.

6. When working with groups of people, do your best to create harmony amongst them. Think of groups of people who harmonise when they sing together and make a wonderful sound. Do your best to cause this to happen with other groups of people, that they create a harmony just being together (this doesn't mean you have to make them sing!). You need to accept everyone's talents so that you all work together to create a kind of unison. As you do this you will find that you heal yourself and that it creates healing within the others. If you can harmonise your minds together, you will be able to focus with greater clarity and bring about changes for the better in your world.

7. Sound. It becomes you to be more aware of sound, its make up and its very being. Remember that 'In the beginning was the word and the word was God' could

be translated as 'In the beginning was the sound and the sound was everything''. Chanting is important to make you a clearer channel to receive new inspirations and higher vibrations.

8. Treat animals with great respect and love. Care for them as they are invaluable teachers and need to be studied with attention.

9. Treat the flora of the planet with love and respect. Protect the plants and learn to communicate with them.

10. Show love, care and respect for the mineral kingdom. Communication with them is as important as it is with plants and animals.

11. Remember that there are realms beyond your own and communication with them is essential so that understanding may come about and you may take up you true role on the planet. At this present time communication with the angelic realm is important, but there are others that you need to become aware of and assist.

I give these guidelines to you as they were given to me. It does not mean you have to live them to the letter, but they are there to remind you that we do have obligations and also that perhaps we could pay more respect to everything around us. It is good to remember this and realize that they are from the perspective of the Angel Princes.

To end this chapter, I am repeating another piece that was given to me by one of the Angel Princes and this is on the subject of love.

'Love is something that many people find difficulty with. Now is the time to let love enter your life. So when you take a deep breath imagine that you are breathing in love. Remember that there are many souls on the Earth that deserve love and do not be afraid to give it. For by giving it, it will be returned to thee and it will be returned to thee more than threefold – for that is the law. To learn love of depth and experience is to know yourself completely and to experience this love you need to be loving of yourself. You need to be secure in your own heart and mind that you have respect for yourself. It is most important that you have respect for yourself, and it is necessary that you create an environment of peace and love around you and include anything that strengthens this atmosphere.

As your self respect and love grows then you can start expressing it in many ways to others. You do not have to speak of it as actions often speak louder than words. Contemplate on this fact, that there are many ways to express love other than speech. Quiet your racing mind and allow yourself to speak the greater truth of love. Now is the time to start living and loving as you have never done before, for most humans on this planet do not truly understand love'.

The Angel Princes have a very special task to do, reminding us to treat each other and all beings with reverence, whether they be plant, animal or mineral. They are doing the best they can for each area to bring everyone who resides there into a new kind of harmony. I urge you all to start working with these incredible beings of light and colour, so that we may bring a new understanding to the human race.

About the author

Carolyn Bowyer was born in St Austell, Cornwall. She was always psychic and got into trouble for it at school. When told on which day sports day would take place, she asked why it would be then, as she knew it would rain! She told them this information and everyone gazed at her oddly! Things worsened when sports day came and it did rain!

Forced to write with her right hand when she was left handed caused her left eye to become crooked, and so she became very shy and reclusive, and was always falling ill.

Carolyn was glad to move at the age of seven to Callington, where she firmly resolved not to tell anyone what she saw or heard with her psychic sense. At age nine her eye was straightened and she began to talk to others again. The warm hearts of the people of Callington enabled her to have more confidence in herself. She worked hard at school, and became top of Callington

Primary school, before moving to Newquay, where she attended the Grammar school.

The fresh coastal air of Newquay helped her become very much healthier and she began to make good friends. She left school with 7 'O' levels and after earning enough to keep herself in spending money for a year, went to train at the now famous Leida Costigan's Henlow Grange Beauty Farm.

Although she encountered many problems during her training, she loved the work and after she had qualified, left to work in Bournemouth. Here she worked for a large Jewish family and learned a lot about their religion, which she found fascinating. However she found she could not bear to be away from her beloved Cornwall, and becoming ill she returned home.

Carolyn worked in a variety of jobs and met many different people. Amongst them was the man who was destined to become her first husband. Carolyn has two daughters from this marriage, Kim born in Cornwall and Nikki born in Malta.

Not long after their return from Malta, the marriage broke up and Carolyn returned to Cornwall with her two children. Having now to support them, she took a job as a receptionist in a refrigeration company where she met her present husband, Bo.

One day walking through Newquay, she woke up in

the library, having no idea how or why she was there. She realized that she had crossed two streets in this state and took it as a sign that she could no longer hide the fact that she was psychic.

Her father was diagnosed with cancer and given three months to live. Carolyn was determined that he would live longer and took him to a healer, who told her that she herself could heal.

At first Carolyn was very sceptical of this, but gradually, as the healer had predicted it would, healing came to her. It enabled her to keep her father alive for a further three years.

Carolyn became a member of the National Federation of Spiritual Healers and passed the criteria to become a fully qualified member. She began training as a medium with Marie Cherrie.

Gradually everything came together and Carolyn started her own business and began to incorporate all her skills together. Two very spiritual teachers, Christine Sapsford and Barbara Sidebottom, taught her aromatherapy. Barbara was to introduce her to the angels. Carolyn became fascinated by this and not long after met up with the Angel Raphael.

Slowly more information came through to her and she began to teach some of the things she had learned to others. In 1991 she was given the suggestion by spirit, that she should start a mind, body and spirit festival. Feeling unable to do this by herself Carolyn met up with Maria Faulkner, and together they started Cornwall New Age Festival.

They started with one day in 1991 and raised over a £1000 for Mount Kailash school for Tibetan children.

Maria backed out in 1993 and Carolyn's husband Bo took her place and they have run it together ever since. It has now grown to four days and is no longer run entirely for charity since Bo was made redundant in 1993. The festival became Bo's business in 1997.

It was in 1997 that Carolyn found she had a spare space for a workshop that was against three very big speakers. She felt it unfair to give it to anyone else, so took the space herself and did a talk on angels, and was surprised to find that 35 people turned up for it! Thus the angel workshops were born. Her daughter Nikki painted the archangels for her and Neil H recorded special music for each angel.

Since then Carolyn has taught workshops all over the country and in Canada and Spain. She now has two grandchildren and still lives in Newquay with her husband and is always fascinated to see what the angels have in store for her next!

Past Life Angels
Discovering your life's master-plan
Jenny Smedley 2nd printing

*Jenny Smedley is Britain's leading authority on past lives.
And it certainly shows in **Past Life Angels**. What a book!
Beautifully written, it's riveting, and thought provoking – I
love its essential premise: having the same spirit guide
for your soul for all eternity. A wonderful read, I can't
recommend it highly enough.* – **Mary Bryce, editor of** Chat

9781905047314/1905047312•208pp £9.99 $19.95

The Angel Connection
Divinity in the new energy
Christina Lunden

*This delightful and enlightening book teaches you how you
may have a personal relationship with your own Angels.
It is a must read for every person who wants to have a
greater understanding of the Angelic relationship that God
has created for them.* – **Nick Bunick, the subject of the
bestselling book**, The Messengers.

9781905047536/1905047533•128pp £11.99 $19.95

Angel Messages
Open your heart to love, and create the life of your
dreams
Jenny Boylan
**These messages offer clarity in times of confusion,
comfort in times of struggle and hope in the pursuit of
ones dreams.**

*Gentle reminders to live the extraordinary life in a mindful
manner… elegantly simple, it can soothe and stir, comfort
and inspire, a book that will be cherished.* – **Wave**

9781903816233/1903816238•333pp•210x135 £14.99 $22.95 cl.

The Fall
The evidence for a Golden Age, 6,000 years of insanity, and the dawning of a new era

STEVE TAYLOR

The Fall *is one of the most notable works of the first years of our century, and I am convinced it will be one of the most important books of the whole century.–*
Elias Capriles, International Journal of Transpersonal Studies

Important and fascinating, highly readable and enlightening.
– Eckhart Tolle

9781905047208/1905047207 • 352pp £12.99 $24.95

Nostradamus
The Illustrated Prophecies

PETER LEMESURIER
2nd printing

A revelation. I am amazed by the translations' objectivity and Lemesurier's refusal to interpret the prophecies beyond what the text itself suggests. The handsomely produced book is a supremely important volume to stock in your store. **– New Age Retailer**

9781903816486/1903816483 • 512pp • 230×153mm • b/w and colour illustrations

£19.99 $29.95 cl.

The Secret History of the West
The influence of secret organisations from the Renaissance to the 20th century

NICHOLAS HAGGER

If you think that the history of Western civilization is all about progressive leaps and bounds, with Utopian visions often ending in wars, then think again. Nicholas Hagger has produced an enticing narrative analysing the roots and histories of large and small revolutions since the Renaissance. **– Nexus**

9781905047048/1905047045 • 592pp • 230×153mm £16.99 $29.95

Sheep
The remarkable story of the humble animal that built the modern world

ALAN BUTLER

The story of the sheep 'is' the story of humanity, a surprisingly exciting and gripping tale that deserves to be told. Spanning a vast period of time, it includes some of the most famous names that have been left to us by history, and many that deserve to better recognised.

9781905047680/1905047681 • 224pp £9.95 $19.95 cl.

The Syndicate
The story of the coming world government

NICHOLAS HAGGER
2nd printing

Finally, a solid book about this pressing matter, and refreshingly without the usual hysteria or excessive speculation. Hagger has done his homework and is initially just concerned with supplying extensive data. Upon this he builds his case: contrary to popular belief, the desire for world domination has never died down. – **Amazon Review**

9781903816851/1903816858 • 456pp • 230×153mm £11.99 $17.95

The Unknown Nostradamus
The true story of his life and work

PETER LEMESURIER

Readers seeking a balanced look at the controversial astrologer will do well to start here. – **Publisher's Weekly**

A "must-read" for anyone seeking to learn more about this remarkable figure... **Midwest Book Review**

9781903816325/1903816327 • 288pp • 230×153mm £17.99 $27.95 cl.
9781903816479/1903816475 £14.99 pb.

Warriors of the Lord
The military orders of Christendom

MICHAEL WALSH

Wonderfully accessible and well written. – **Publisher's Weekly**

Offers great breadth of knowledge in an enormously accessible and straightforward fashion ...an agreeable and satisfying introduction. – **Library Journal**

9781842981078/1842981072 • 260pp • 280×210mm • full colour
£19.99 cl.

The 7 Aha!s of Highly Enlightened Souls
How to free yourself from ALL forms of stress

MIKE GEORGE
7th printing

A very profound, self empowering book. Each page bursting with wisdom and insight. One you will need to read and reread over and over again! **... Paradigm Shift**

I totally love this book, a wonderful nugget of inspiration. – **PlanetStarz**

9781903816318/1903816319 • 128pp • 190×135mm £5.99 $11.95

God Calling
A devotional diary

A. J. RUSSELL
46th printing

"When supply seems to have failed, you must know that it has not done so. But you must look around to see what you can give away. Give away something."
One of the best-selling devotional books of all time, with over 6 million copies sold.

9781905047420/1905047428 • 280pp • 135×95mm • US rights sold
£7.99 cl.

The Goddess, the Grail and the Lodge
The Da Vinci Code and the real origins of religion
ALAN BUTLER
5th printing

This book rings through with the integrity of sharing time-honoured revelations. As a historical detective, following a golden thread from the great Megalithic cultures, Alan Butler vividly presents a compelling picture of the fight for life of a great secret and one that we simply can't afford to ignore. **– From the foreword by Lynn Picknett & Clive Prince**

9781903816691/1903816696 • **360pp** • **230×152mm £12.99 $19.95**

The Heart of Tantric Sex
A unique guide to love and sexual fulfilment
DIANA RICHARDSON
5th printing

The art of keeping love fresh and new long after the honeymoon is over. Tantra for modern Western lovers adapted in a practical, refreshing and sympathetic way. One of the most revolutionary books on sexuality ever written. ... **Ruth Ostrow, News Ltd**

9781903816370/1903816378 • **260pp** • **b/w+colour illustrations £19.95 $29.95**

I Am With You
The best-selling modern inspirational classic
JOHN WOOLLEY
14th printing hardback

Will bring peace and consolation to all who read it. **– Cardinal Cormac Murphy-O'Connor**

9780853053415/0853053413 • **280pp** • **150×100mm £9.99 cl.**

4th printing paperback

9781903816998/1903816998 • **280pp** • **150x100mm £6.99 $12.95**

O

is a symbol of the world,
of oneness and unity. O Books
explores the many paths of whole-
ness and spiritual understanding which
different traditions have developed down
the ages. It aims to bring this knowledge in
accessible form, to a general readership, pro-
viding practical spirituality to today's seekers.

For the full list of over 200 titles covering:
ACADEMIC/THEOLOGY • ANGELS • ASTROLOGY/
NUMEROLOGY • BIOGRAPHY/AUTOBIOGRAPHY
• BUDDHISM/ENLIGHTENMENT • BUSINESS/LEADERSHIP/
WISDOM • CELTIC/DRUID/PAGAN • CHANNELLING
• CHRISTIANITY; EARLY • CHRISTIANITY; TRADITIONAL
• CHRISTIANITY; PROGRESSIVE • CHRISTIANITY;
DEVOTIONAL • CHILDREN'S SPIRITUALITY • CHILDREN'S
BIBLE STORIES • CHILDREN'S BOARD/NOVELTY • CREATIVE
SPIRITUALITY • CURRENT AFFAIRS/RELIGIOUS • ECONOMY/
POLITICS/SUSTAINABILITY • ENVIRONMENT/EARTH
• FICTION • GODDESS/FEMININE • HEALTH/FITNESS
• HEALING/REIKI • HINDUISM/ADVAITA/VEDANTA
• HISTORY/ARCHAEOLOGY • HOLISTIC SPIRITUALITY
• INTERFAITH/ECUMENICAL • ISLAM/SUFISM
• JUDAISM/CHRISTIANITY • MEDITATION/PRAYER
• MYSTERY/PARANORMAL • MYSTICISM • MYTHS
• POETRY • RELATIONSHIPS/LOVE • RELIGION/
PHILOSOPHY • SCHOOL TITLES • SCIENCE/
RELIGION • SELF-HELP/PSYCHOLOGY
• SPIRITUAL SEARCH • WORLD
RELIGIONS/SCRIPTURES • YOGA

Please visit our website,
www.O-books.net